Dominican Engagement with the World

Edited by Hilary Dominic Regan

Dominican Engagement with the World

An Ongoing Process of Prophetic Dynamism

Edited by Hilary Dominic Regan

THEOLOGY
2023

InterfaceTheology:
Incorporating *Sapientia et Sciencia* and in association with *Wort und Antwort* (Germany)
Volume 8, Number 2, 2023

Editorial Board
Revd Dr John Capper, Stirling College, University of Divinity, Melbourne.
Rev Dr Ulrich Engel OP, Institut M-Dominique Chenu, Berlin.
Dr Janina Hiebel, Yarra Theological Union, University of Divinity, Melbourne.
Dr Philip Kariatlis, St Andrews Greek Orthodox Theological College, Sydney.
Rev Dr Dorothy Lee, Trinity College, University of Divinity, Melbourne.
Dr Mark O'Brien OP, Emeritus, Catholic Theological College, University of Divinity, Melbourne.
Rev Dr Richard Ousnworth OP, Blackfriars Hall, Oxford.
Rev Dr Kris Sonek OP, Catholic Theological College, University of Divinity, Melbourne.

Editorial Manager
Mr Hilary Regan, Publisher, ATF Press Publishing Group, PO Box 234, Brompton SA, 5007, Australia.
Email: hdregan@atf.org.au

International Reference Group
Rev Dr Vicky Balabanksi, Uniting College for Leadership and Theology, Adelaide, Australia.
Rev Dr Darren Dias OP, University of St Michael's College, University of Toronto, Canada.
Rev Dr Thomas Eggensperger OP, Institut M-Dominique Chenu, Berlin, Germany.
Rev Dr Ted Peters, Pacific Lutheran Theological School, Berkley, USA.
Rev Dr Murray Rae, University of Otago, Dunedin, New Zealand.

Subscription rates
Print Local: Individual Aus $55, Institutions Aus $65.
Overseas: Individuals US $60, Institutions US $65.

Interface Theology is a biannual refereed journal of theology published in print, Epub and PDF by ATF Press Publishing Group.
The journal is a scholarly ecumenical and interdisciplinary publication, aiming to serve the church and its mission, promoting a broad-based interpretation of Christian theology within a trinitarian context, encouraging dialogue between Christianity and other faiths, and exploring the interface between faith and culture. It is published in English for an international audience.

ISSN 2203-465X
Cover art work Yvonne Ashby

978-1-923006-42-3   Soft
978-1-923006-43-0   Hard
978-1-923006-44-7   Epub
978-1-923006-45-4   PDF

An imprint of ATF Theology part of the ATF Press Publishing Group which is owned by
ATF (Australia) Ltd.
PO Box 234,
Brompton, SA, 5007
Australia
www.atfpress.com
Making a lasting impact

InterfaceTheology 8/2 2023

Table of Contents

1. Editorial — vii
   Hilary Regan

2. Study as Spiritual Comfort: On the relationship between theology and piety in the Dominican Order' — 1
   Ulrich Engel OP

3. 'A Most Cultured Lady, a Scholar in the Best Sense . . . ': Mother Mary Columba (Marianne) Boylan OP—1847–1910 — 9
   Gabrielle Kelly OP

4. Homily at the Requiem Mass in Paris for Nicolas-Jean Sed OP — 21
   Eric de Clermont-Tonnerre OP

5. The Architecture or Arrangement of the Psalter: A Proposal — 25
   Mark O'Brien OP

6. Dominican Spirituality: Prophetic Dynamism in a Creative Engagement with the World — 45
   Erik Borgman OPL

7. Thomas Aquinas and a Vast Universe — 59
   Thomas O'Meara OP

8. New Theological Tendencies — 67
   Pietro Parente

9. A Brief Note on Parente, Garrigou Lagrange and Chenu — 71
   Alessandro Cortesi, OP

10. Contributors — 75

Editorial

Much has been written over the years on the history of the Dominican Order, of its founder (St Dominic), its many saints and blesseds, key historical figures, different institutions, and its mission and activities. St Dominic in founding the Order of Preachers left nothing written, and used the Rule written by another (St Augustine's) when founding his religious order.

Within the Catholic world there are many spiritual and theological traditions that have a place in the call to follow in the footsteps of Jesus. In the realm of spirituality there are a variety of schools following the life and writings of a number of people. The Spiritual Exercises of St Ignatius are one such very well-known and followed example which has been the model for many religious institutes and organisations of spiritual renewal. The Dominican 'way' has always been a less structured and defined spirituality. The Dominican 'way' is also an acceptance that it is but one way among many ways to follow Jesus Christ. It is to some extent illusive, hard to define or encapsulate in one word, one line or one phrase. However, by looking with a discerning frame of reference at the tradition that has developed over the last 800 plus years one can, perhaps, define certain threads, certain key elements, certain constants, that shape and define the Dominican 'way'. The motto of 'Veritas'—truth—has been often quoted as the defining word, but as like so many one word mottos it needs clarification, explanation, defining, distilling to meet an ever changing context of situations, contexts, challenges and needs.

The essays in this volume examine various aspects of Dominican life. There are essays on prayer, spirituality, historical and biblical pieces as well as a piece on the work on the work of publishing by Dominicans. The contributors come from different parts of the world and reflect different vocations within the Order.

The overarching theme in the volume is that the Dominican tradition is one of dynamic engagement, a dynamic engagement with the world, with issues, ideas, concepts, topics, biblical studies, theology, philosophy, social analysis and history in whatever activity is undertaken. It is a process, one which is never static but always searching and calling for new ideas, new expressions, new ways to look at and to respond to the situation/s in front of us, and also importantly to make some response to the needs of the time as they confront us. It is the following of an intuition, a thought an insight, to see where it leads, to look at the context/s, all the twists of possible interpretations, understandings and to come to certain decisions in how to frame this and talk about it. At the same time, it is not just a study of a certain topic (theological or otherwise), issue, idea, event, institution. It is not just an investigation for its own sake, but at its core to take another step. It is a handing on, a transmitting, a passing on to others of what has been learnt, discovered, engaged with, grappled with, teased out, developed, and in that it is an addition to a growing, developing body of knowledge, of what we call as a tradition.

That process, in part is what has been described by some as the Salamanca Process.[1] It is prophetic not so much as a 'foretelling the future', but a standing back, looking at situations, topics, themes, events, institutions, people, actions, ideas and situations to try to detail, outline, define, and attempt to interpret what is being witnessed, described and experienced. It is dynamic in so far it adds to a body of knowledge, ideas, interpretations and is always open to new analyses and to reinterpretation.

Once again, this dynamic process is not unique to just the Dominican tradition, as others could also claim it, or do the same thing without naming it. Nor has it always been undertaken perfectly, or to its best, by all those who are part of the tradition (indeed there are times in history where it has been undertaken better than in others), but it is perhaps always that 'something', that those who follow the tradition can stand back, recognise, and, recognise that 'something', the various elements, and they say 'yes, that is the Dominican 'way'.

These essays then are one way of providing some examples of this 'way', a way of an ongoing process of prophetic dynamism.

Hilary Dominic Regan

---

1. See among other titles *Dominicans and Human Rights* (Adelaide: ATF Press, 2016).

Study as a spiritual comfort
On the relationship between theology and piety in the Dominican Order

Ulrich Engel OP

In the former Dominican convent of San Marco in Florence—now a museum—there is a well-known, frequently reproduced fresco depicting St Dominic by Fra Angelico OP. The picture in cell 7 shows the founder of the order below a depiction of the mockery of Christ. His posture is concentrated. On his lap lies an open book. His gaze is on the book. He reads. Is Dominic studying here or praying? In any case, he sits.

Kneeling or sitting theology?

When it comes to the relationship between theology and piety, Hans Urs von Balthasar's word of 'kneeling theology' is often and first quoted. Almost half a century ago, the Swiss theologian wrote, with his gaze firmly fixed on the Fathers of the Church and their time: 'At that time it was known what theological style is: the self-evident unity as well as the attitude of faith and knowledge as well as objectivity and reverence. Theology, as long as it was a theology of the saints, was a praying, a kneeling theology. That is why their prayer yield, their fruitfulness for prayer, their prayer-generating power have been so incalculable.' The echo of this thesis resonates to this day,[1] for example where Pope Benedict XVI, for example, felt motivated by the words quoted to 'reconsider the right significance of research in theology'.[2]

---

1. Hans Urs Balthasar, *Verbum Caro* (Sketches on Theology 1), Einsiedeln ³1990, 224; originally published under the title: 'Theology and Holiness', in: *Food and Wisdom* 3 (1948), S. 881–897.
2. Benedict XVI, Message to the participants of the international conference on the occasion of the 100th birthday of the Swiss theologian Hans Urs von Balthasar:

What was Balthasar's contribution on the relationship between *theology and holiness* about? Already in the opening sentence he clearly marks his point of view: 'There is hardly an event in the history of Catholic theology that has received less attention and yet deserves more attention than the fact that there have been few holy theologians since high scholasticism'. This expresses the view of a history of decay of theology: where its representatives once appeared sacred, their modern epigones hardly deserve the predicate anymore. Such a theological historical evaluation, as presented by Balthasar here, does not come across as ‚innocent'. Rather, it proves to be guided by interest, as it plays off the praying theology of the saints against the scientific theology (of the unholy) together with its own rationality: 'At some point the turn from kneeling theology to seated theology happened (. . .). "Scientific" theology becomes more unobstructural and thus more inexperienced in the tone with which one should talk about the sacred.'[3, 4]

It is hardly surprising that critical voices were raised against this rationality-sceptical attitude. Paradigmatically mentioned in this context is man Dominikus Koster. The dogmatist teaching in Walberberg vehemently opposed the devaluation of modern scientific theology, which in his opinion was clearly evident in von Balthasar's draft.[5] Koster's objection concerned above all a too little critical reception of fathers' theology (to the detriment of school theology).

In my opinion, however, the criticism must be more fundamental. For insofar as Balthasar is not able to reconcile reason (scientificness) and faith (sacred), his concept of theology is problematic overall. As a result, von Balthasar sacrifices the conceptual-reflexive speech about

---

www.vatican.va/holy_father/benedict_xvi/messages/pont-messages/2005/documents/hf_benxvi_mes_20051006_von-balthasar_ge.html [Call: 11.7.2022].
3. Balthasar, Verbum Caro, loc. cit., S. 195, 224.
4. Balthasar, Verbum Caro, loc. cit., S. 195.., 224.
5. *Cf* Mannes Dominikus Koster, Theology and Holiness. Eine kritische Entgegenung, in: The New Order 4 (1950), S. 113-121.—About person and work cf. Ortto Hermann Pesch, mannes Dominikus Koster OP (1901-1981). Church as "People of God", in: Thgrannies Eggensperger / Ulrich Engel (Hrsg.), "Mutig in die Zukunft!"Dominikanische Beiträge zum Vaticanum II (Dominikanische Quellen und Zeugnisse 10), Leipzig 2007, S. 191-228; Piotr Napiwodski, An Ecclesiology in Becoming. Mannes Dominikus Koster und sein Beitrag zum theologischen Verständnis der Kirche, Freiburg/Ue. 2005 [eThesis], under: https://folia.unifr.ch/global/documents/299854 [Call: 11.7.2022].

God (theology) to the speech on God (prayer). The scientific theology denounced for its alleged rationalism must then serve as a negative distorted image of true, i.e. pious theology. Ultimately, we are dealing with von Balthasar with a rather dualistic conception.

Study as a spiritual comfort

In order to escape this still omnipresent danger of dualism—here secular science, there godly piety—I take a different approach: with the tradition of the order of preachers. Symbolic of this is the image of The sitting meditating/studying Dominic of Fra Angelico. My determined interest is to 'explore the paths of a scientific-academic and a life-world-religious order (. . .) to stick together and thus work against ruinous separation efforts'.[6]

In the study concept of the Dominicans, science and piety were closely related from the beginning. Ulrich Horst has examined this connection using the example of the text[7] *Contra impugnantes Dei cultum et religionem* by Thomas Aquinas, completed in 1256. The Opusculum, originally an ad *hoc* occasional pamphlet reacting to the Paris Mendicant and University Controversy, was soon received by the preacher brothers of the 13th century as a program on their own behalf. Thomas succeeds there 'in a deeper determination of the relationship between study and preaching and a strongly conceived assignment of a scholastically operated theology to the conventual *vita religiosa*. Science and piety, once perceived as tension or even as opposition, are now strictly related to each other in order to cross-fertilize each other'. Although study is directed towards the Order's goal of preaching God's mercy for the salvation of humankind and in

---

6. 26 years of basic theological course—a retrospective. Interview with T.R. Peters on 13.11.2003, in: Bertil Langenohl / Christian Große Rüschkamp (ed.), Wozu Theologie? Anstiftungen aus der praktische Fundamentaltheologie von Tiemo Rainer Peters (Religion—Geschichte—Gesellschaft 32), Münster 2005, S. 77–84, here S. 81f.
7. On the significance and organisation of studies in the Order of Preachers cf. basic M.-Dominique Chenu, The Saulchoir. A school of theology. Translated from the French by Michael Lauble, hrsg. by Christian Bauer, Thgrannies Eggensperger and Ulrich Engel (Chenu Collection Bd. 2), Berlin 2003, bes. S. 54–88; Henri-MArie Féret, Vie intellectuelle et vie scholaire dans l›ordre des Frères Prêcheurs, in: Archives d›histoire dominicaine 1946, vol. 1, S. 5–37.

this respect (like the observances and vows) is to be regarded ‚only' as a means of pastoral care[8, 9] *(cura animarum)*—it is also 'an integral part of monastic spirituality'.[10]

More precisely, Thomas defines the study as a 'spiritual consolation' *(spiritual solatium)*. This means: 'The religious existence of the preacher's brother is no longer based solely on[11] *meditatio* and *lectio*, but also on *disputatio*, i.e. on a theology that had become common at universities and colleges in the meantime.' This marks a monastic life practice that radically departs from all "anti-intellectual tendencies" of the monastic-feudal tradition. What is new about the Order of the Preacher Brothers is the close connection between traditional piety (in the form of contemplation and reading of Scripture) on the one hand and theological intellectuality (with scholastic disputation) on the other. In this context, Ulrich Horst recalls that, in the opinion of the first generations of preacher brothers, the study was of a religious character. This is made clear, among other things, in the fact that a brother was entrusted with the exercise of the theological Magisterium "for the forgiveness of sins"[12, 13] *(in remission peccatorum)*.[14]

Process of continuous incarnation

In the wake of Thomas Aquinas, I do not understand faith *(fides)* and reason *(ratio)* as two contradictory worlds. I recognize the often missed link between faith and reason or piety and scientific theology in the event of the incarnation. This does not primarily represent a specific content of the theological statement. Rather, I understand

---

8. Ulrich Horst Ways to follow Christ. The Theology of the Order according to Thomas Aquinas (Quellen und Forschungen zur Geschichte des Dominikanerordens N.F. 12), Berlin 2006, S. 20. In principle, see also Thgrannies Eggensperger, Paths to Succession. Ulrich Horst examines the theology of the order according to Thomas Aquinas, in: *Oriented▪ Vocational training* 70 (2006), S. 256–259.
9. Cf. Free Constitutionum et Ordinationum Fratrum Ordinis Praedicatorum, ed. from Bruno CadoréRome 2019, Constitutio Fundamentalis, § 4.
10. Horst Ways to follow Christ, loc. cit., S. 21.
11. Cf. Contra impugnantes Dei cultum et religionem, ed. Hyacinthe-François Dondaine (Editio Leonina theft. 41), Roma 1970, A 5—A 181, yesterday A 51f. (Prologus).
12. Horst, Ways to follow Christ, loc. cit., S. 75.
13. Ibid. S. 34.
14. Cf. ibid. Note 30.

Incarnation following Marie-Dominique Chenu as a theological form of thought. "Without a doubt, Christianity is the mystery of Christ, who lives, dies and rises in me; but how did this mystery unfold? In an incarnation, i.e. in a coming of God into time and history (. . .). As a consequence, the coming of Christ, or rather: the time between the two arrivals of Christ, namely the historical arrival and the end-time, is the transformation of the world".[15, 16]

Because the incarnated Word of God has become temporalized in history, it can and must become flesh again and again in this very story. A theological reflection rooted in this incarnation can only be a way of thinking that starts from the politically, socially and culturally concrete in all its historical forms and finds in it ever new appropriate forms of expression for God's Word. Theological practice thus determined has its place in the Church as the People of God: "Insofar as this divine Word is entrusted to the Church, she shares in the claim of each new incarnation." According to Chenu's conviction, the incarnation of God did not happen once and for all in Judea 2,000 years ago, but continues throughout history.[17, 18]

In theological reflection, the Incarnation is realized in two ways: as *an incarnation in terms* of the Word of God—for example in dogmatic sentences—as well as as an incarnation of the Word of God *in the theologian*, who thinks his/her faith back and forth on the historical, social and economic conditions. The theological hermeneutics of the incarnation firmly believes in the presence of God in the historically concrete circumstances of the world, which is certainly often hidden. In the face of the other, she seeks to perceive him as an other and thus as a person with his own dignity. In him he recognizes the face of Jesus Christ. In this sense, I understand Chenu's thesis: "The theologian is a believer." As such, it reflects the pre-gift of revelation that has been handed down to us as the Word of God in human

---

15. Cf. see Ulrich Angel Theologale Mystik im Konflikt. Marie-Dominique Chenu and the basic intuitions of his theology, in: ders., God of man. Wegmarken dominikanischer Theologie, Ostfildern 2010, 145–165.
16. Marie-Dominique Chenu, The Word of God. II: L'Évangile dans les temps, Paris 1964, S. 114.
17. Ibid.
18. Cf. Christophe F. Potworowski, Contemplation and Incarnation. The Theology of Marie-Dominique Chenu (McGill-Queen's Studies in the History of Ideas theft. 33), Montreal u. a. 2001, S. XV.

words. It is the task of such a process of knowledge, which is based on faith and at the same time realized in concrete history, "to find God's hidden presence and (. . .) to show that the unity of reality we long for is already given, albeit in a hidden way." Only if one acknowledges the historical evidence of this world of ours with its differences and ruptures and believes in its fundamental god-will, one can see God and Christ again and again from their innermost being.[19, 20]

Study of the Word of God—Study of the World

In the tradition of the Order of Preachers, study always means the study of the Word of God: "Brother Dominic often warned and encouraged the brothers of the Order orally and in his letters that they should always study in the New and Old Testaments." However, such a study is not necessarily exclusively exegetical or biblically oriented. Nor is it necessarily focused solely on the biblical texts. Starting from the traditionally very strong emphasis in the Dominican Order on the incarnation of the Word of God into the human-worldly conditions, the study of the Word of God is to be understood as the intellectual confrontation with all the realities occurring in this world. According to Thomas Aquinas, theology speaks not only about religion or about God as an object of human knowledge, but about[21] *everything*—under the aspect of God *(sub ratione Dei)*. Thus, insofar as God as well as the created reality in its relationship to the divine origin form the subject of theology, non-theological studies are also legitimized. Accordingly, Thomas vehemently defended the thesis that the religious not only had to do theology, but should also turn to the so-called secular sciences.[22]

It is surprising that Thomas granted the Mendicants in general and the Dominicans in particular the preoccupation with secular knowledge. For the recommendation of the Aquinas at that time was (still) in

---

19. Chenu, The Saulchoir, loc. cit., S. 123.
20. ERik Borgman, Theology: Science at the Borders, in: Concilium (D) 42 (2006), S. 248–258, here S. 251f.
21. Acta canonizationis S. Dominici, ed. by Angelus Walz, in: Monumenta historica S. P. N. Dominici, Fasc. II (MOPH 16), Roma 1935, 123–167, No. 29, here quoted. to: Vladimir J. Koudelka (Hrsg.), Dominikus (Gotteserfahrung und Weg in die Welt), Olten—Freiburg/Br. 1983, S. 181.
22. Cf. STh I 1, 7 c.

contradiction to an arrangement of the constitutions of the preacher brothers, which excluded the secular sciences from the study program and forbade the reading of books of the pagans and philosophers. It is essentially the merit of Albertus Magnus "to give philosophy the space in the study of the Dominicans that it had to occupy in order to enable a real synthesis of Greek-Arab science and Christian wisdom." The advocacy of a preoccupation with secular knowledge advocated by Thomas and Albert finally established itself as the standard in the Order of Preachers. From this point of view, Dominican study means reading and trying to understand the text of the world.[23, 24]

Intellectual poverty and theological critique

At the same time, the study of the incarnated Word teaches intellectual poverty before the mystery of the ever greater and, above all, ever different God. "Theology has always had to deal with the fact that its subject—in classical theology this is God—in our limited attempts to rationalize reality exceeds our comprehension." Thomas also pointed this out: "Only then do we truly know God if we believe that he is above all that man can think of God." And: "(. . .) we are more likely to experience what God is not than what He is. So if we use images of things that are further removed from God, we become more aware of how high God is above everything we can say or think of Him."[25, 26, 27]

Such intellectual poverty, however, does not float in a vacuum. It must be grounded in the world of life, i.e. it needs a place. "Dominican theology began when Dominic got off his horse and became a poor preacher. The intellectual poverty of a Thomas is inseparable from his choice of an order of poor preachers."[28]

---

23. Cf. Horst Ways to follow Christ, loc. cit., S. 69f.
24. Wage Senner, Johannes von Sterngassen OP und sein Sentenzenkommentar. Part I: Study (Sources and Research on the History of the Dominican Order N.F. Bd. 4), Berlin 1995, S. 113.
25. Borgman, Theology, loc. cit., S. 255.
26. ScG I, 5.
27. STh I, 1, 9 ad 3.
28. Timothy Radcliffe, The Source of Hope. Study and proclamation of the Guten Nachricht, in: ders., Gemeinschaft im Dialog. Ermutigung zum Ordensleben, hrsg. by Thgrannies Eggensperger and Ulrich Engel (Dominikanische Quellen und Zeugnisse 2), Leipzig 2001, S. 65–96, here S. 76. Cf. also Ulrich Angel, sermon "from below". On the charisma of Dominican spirituality, in: Geist

Accordingly, a theologically prepared intellectuality entails a willingness and ability to perceive, which is based on the Jesus Beatitude of those who are seeing eyes (cf. Mt 13:16; Luke 10:23). From this arises both the mystical and the political character of theological reflection. After all, "Jesus did not teach a mysticism of closed eyes, but a kind of perceptual mysticism, a mysticism of open eyes, which see more and not less than others, which above all make invisible, inconvenient suffering visible".[29]

A theology thus incarnated into the contradictory realities of history and society, alert to the signs of the times, aims at the preaching of joy and hope. It is incumbent on the theologians to be present in the places of destruction and suffering, of violence and hatred, and "to transform these places so that they become places of joyful encounter instead of violence, mutual recognition instead of hatred. If we are to bring *Gaudium et spes*, then we must be present in these places of, *luctus et angor'—,sorrow and pain*."[30]

Here the intellectuality of theological as well as non-theological studies reaches its goal—namely to lead us scientists ourselves to a conversion in which "our false images of God are destroyed so that we can approach the mystery." In its critical potential, theology must thus turn against all absolutes, delusions and fundamentalisms, especially in the name of religion–[31] *ad extra* as criticism of religion and *ad intra* as criticism of the church! In this twofold critique, theological rationality and practical piety come together: as spiritual comfort for the world.[32]

Translated by Victor Pfitzner.

---

and life 79 (2006), S. 161–169; Thgrannies Eggensperger, Thomas Aquinas and the "evangelical poverty". Zur Theologiegeschichte eines aktuelle Themas, in: Oriented▪ Vocational training 58 (1994), S. 33–35.

29. Johann Baptist Metz, so many faces, so many questions. Lateinamerika mit den Augen eines europäischen Theologen, in: ders. / HYears-Eckehard Bahr, eyes for others. Lateinamerika—eine theologische Erfahrung, Munich 1991, S. 11–61, here S. 53.
30. Timothy Radcliffe, Zur Freiheit der Theologie. Greeting to the colloquium on the occasion of the 35th anniversary of the journal "Concilium", in: ders., Gemeinschaft im Dialog, loc. cit., S. 285–290, here S. 289.
31. Ders., The Source of Hope, loc. cit., S. 76.
32. Cf. Anddmund Arens, Der Beitrag der Theologie zur universitären Bildung, in: ders. u. a., Geistesgegenwärtig. Zur Zukunft universitärer Bildung, Lucerne 2003, S. 85–106, here S. 99.

'A most cultured lady, a scholar in the best sense...' Mother Mary Columba (Marianne) Boylan OP—1847–1910[1]

Gabrielle Kelly OP

Introduction

In September 1868, just thirty-two years after proclamation of the colony, at the request of Bishop Sheil, a group of seven young Dominican sisters led by Mother Mary Teresa Moore left their convent at Cabra, Dublin on a mission to establish the first Catholic secondary school for girls in Adelaide, South Australia.[2] Six years later, Mother M Columba Boylan, and companion, M Catherine Kavanagh,[3] were despatched from the same Dublin convent to help salvage the near-total collapse of the Adelaide mission. That Mother Columba was able to lead her community, from troubled beginnings, to develop a well-respected and expanded educational mission in the colony over the following couple of decades is testament to her qualities as leader and educator. Her manner of doing so left for those who followed a fine example of the Dominican charism in action in an emerging educational context in a developing new society.

---

1. This paper was first prepared as a staff formation resource for two Colleges of Dominican tradition now under the auspices of Dominican Education Australia. M Columba Boylan was the second formally appointed Prioress of St Mary's Convent, Franklin Street (1875–1885), and founding Prioress, St Mary's Dominican Convent, Cabra (1886–1896, 1899–1905). Both schools were originally known as St. Mary's Dominican Convent, at each location. From 1968, the Franklin Street school became St Mary's College; around the early 1970s, Cabra was formally named as Cabra Dominican College.
2. Colony proclaimed on 28 December, 1836, when the first British settlers arrived at Holdfast Bay. A site was selected twelve kilometres inland 'on the bank of a beautiful stream . . .' for the main settlement. Colonel William Light, Surveyor General, commenced town plan survey of 1,042 acres of still scrub-covered land on 11/1/1837.
3. Accompanied also by Sr Stephana Waldron, returning to Adelaide after accompanying a pioneer sister who returned to Ireland.

Early colonial context

While schooling of any kind was still in its infancy, from the outset[4] the bishops had been proactive in encouraging elementary education for Catholic children.[5] But, unlike the other colonies, in 1851 the government of South Australia withdrew financial assistance from denominational schools. The second bishop, Patrick Geoghegan, denounced government schools as 'a work of proselytism' for Protestantism and rallied the Catholic community to action.[6] The Sisters of St Joseph were founded in 1866 to provide elementary schooling for children of working class families, but this did not meet the 'real need for the church to provide for higher study',[7] particularly for older girls, for whom there was no adequate, easily accessible regular provision for schooling of any kind.[8]

It was the third Bishop of Adelaide (1866-1872), Laurence Bonaventure Sheil, who was concerned to provide such schooling for girls. Acutely aware 'of the great want of superior[9] schools in our diocese, especially for the female portion of the young', he had travelled to Ireland to seek 'a first rate teaching order' to fill that need.[10] At the welcome in Adelaide in December 1868, Sheil expressed pleasure at having been able to enlist the Cabra, Dublin sisters, whose reputation of 'signal pre-eminence in the education of the higher classes of female society' preceded them.[11] In February 1869, in Franklin Street west, adjacent to the colony's first Catholic church, they opened St Mary's, a school for 'young ladies' (boarders admitted in the following year) and in October a lower fee 'intermediate' school for day pupils, both

---

4. The Diocese of Adelaide was established in 1842.
5. Helen Northey, *Living the Truth – The Dominican Sisters in South Australia, 1868-1958* (Adelaide: Holy Cross Congregation of Dominican Sisters SA, 1999), 32–33.
6. Margaret Press, *From our Broken Toil* (Adelaide: Catholic Archdiocese of Adelaide, 1986), 134–5.
7. Northey, *Living the Truth* . . ., 36.
8. Gabrielle Kelly, 'The Dominican Sisters' Contribution to Education for Girls in Early S.A.', M Ed course work paper, University of Adelaide, November 1989, 10–11.
9. 'Superior' denoted secondary education including a foreign language. Cf Northey, *Living the Truth*, 36, ftnt 16.
10. Francis Sheil, Pastoral Letter, July 1867, *Southern Cross & Catholic Herald*, 20 November, 1867. See also Northey, *Living the Truth*. . ., 35–38.
11. *Southern Cross and Catholic Herald*, 20 December, 1868.

girls and boys. Later, they took over operation of a free poor school, previously conducted by the Sisters of St Joseph.[12]

Sadly, the pioneer sisters encountered many difficulties. They found themselves in a small Catholic community, riven with clerical conflict, lacking sound leadership, and struggling with few resources to establish itself in a strongly Protestant colony. Though they made a sound beginning,[13] increasing enrolments,[14] heavy workloads, unrelenting tension and their own shortcomings, exacerbated by the failing health and eventual death of Mother Teresa in January 1873, led to the near collapse of the mission.[15] An urgent plea was made to Cabra, Dublin for more help.[16] At Cardinal Cullen's urging, the Dublin prioress agreed to send M Columba Boylan and M Catherine Kavanagh, noting that Cabra made 'great sacrifices' in sending two sisters recognised as among their best and most capable.[17]

Mother Mary Columba (Marianne) Boylan OP

Marianne Boylan, an only child, was born on 11 June 1847, in Carbury, County Kildare, in Ireland. Her mother died in childbirth and her father, Patrick, who did not marry again, died when she was eight or nine years old. Marianne was cared for by Maddie Flanagan, her mother's sister. In 1859, they sent her, aged twelve or thirteen, to the Dominican boarding school (Immaculata) in Cabra, Dublin. On finishing school, Marianne entered the Dominican novitiate on 6 January 1864, receiving the religious Habit eight months later on 4 August. However, she could not make profession before ceding

---

12. Northey, *Living the Truth* . . ., 5.
13. E.g. The 1870 end of year display at St Mary's attracted 'the highest encomiums . . .upon the management of the institution' . . . a 'blessing' to the whole Adelaide community, 'not confined to any particular class . . .' (i.e. including children from Catholic, Protestant and Jewish families)—cf *South Australian Chronicle & Weekly Mail* (Adelaide), 24 December 1870, 12–13.
14. Enrolments had grown from 20 on 2/2/1869 to 150 by 1873. Cf Northey, *Living the Truth*, 47; AHC, 28.)
15. To add to the sense of flux, Bishop Sheil, who had invited them to Adelaide, died in March 1872.
16. In the interim, two experienced sisters from the Maitland Dominican Community (NSW) came to provide stabilising support for some months in the early part of 1874. Cf Northey, *Living the Truth* . . ., 71–73.
17. Northey, *Living the Truth* . . ., Chapter Three, 75–76.

her sizeable inheritance to the Flanagan family, and this could not be done before she came of age. As a result, Marianne remained in the novitiate for a further two to three years, acting more-or-less as Assistant Novice Mistress until she could make profession, as Sister Mary Columba, on 15 August 1869. Her leadership gifts were already recognised for she was then appointed Mistress of Schools,[18] a position she held for the next five years until she was sent to South Australia in 1874 'to take the vacant office of Prioress'.[19] On 5 January 1875, she arrived in Adelaide where she would spend the next thirty-five years until her death on 3 May, 1910. On the day following arrival, M Columba was confirmed Prioress by Bishop Reynolds. The fact that for the next twenty-seven years, except between 1896–99 when she was sub-Prioress, the sisters, by special dispensation, six times re-elected Mother Columba as Prioress is evidence of the value placed upon her stabilising leadership and competent management. Yet in hindsight that record poses a critical question: was it in the ultimate best interests of building up a robustly interdependent community for M Columba to acquiesce, on *all* those occasions, in delaying the emergence and formation of leadership capacities in others?[20]

Mother Columba's contribution to Catholic life and education in Adelaide

A century later, a scholarly study concludes that M Columba made a 'substantial and significant' contribution to Catholic life and education in Adelaide.[21] Justification for that assessment is evident in the quality of the educational program over which she presided, the success and expansion of the schools, and her personal reputation among those who knew her.

---

18. In the 20th century, and probably late 19th, the office, Mistress of Schools, meant being in charge of boarders, as well as teaching. Email communication, 25/9/21, Maris Stella McKeown OP, Archivist, Cabra, Dublin.
19. Holy Cross Congregation Archives, M Columba Boylan personal file and Obituary. Details also from hand-written pencil entries in Notes for the Annals 1868–1934-43, exercise book, pp 15a, 16a, Series 031.
20. Northey, *Living the Truth . . .*, 77–78, 87.
21. Northey, *Living the Truth . . .*, 123.

Quality of the educational program

The program brought to Adelaide in 1868 replicated the 'pre-eminent' Cabra Dublin tradition which was distinguished by two key features: the 'absolute importance' of *higher* education for girls—staying at school for 'a sufficient time' was expressly encouraged; and the quality of the program offered. This was marked by the high value placed on literary culture, breadth of knowledge and sound scholarship. Aiming for a balanced formation of hearts and souls as well as minds, the curriculum included grammar, geography, history, mathematics, botany, astronomy and foreign languages, as well as music, drama, art and physical education. As educators, the sisters were guided by their 1843 Constitution which emphasised the great importance of Christian education because of its eternal as well as temporal consequences.[22] Their primary responsibility, in 'justice and charity' was to do all in their power to promote wholesome formation of their pupils. As examples of faith, they were to respect each person, for the 'rich and the poor bear . . . the same image of God'. They should let no field of knowledge 'be undervalued' and pay 'zealous attention' to their own continuing studies; and in the 'spirit of progress', for which Cabra Dublin was renowned, they should strive to adopt the 'best methods', aim for the 'highest standards'.[23] It is not by chance that these values echo emphases intrinsic to the spirituality of Dominic's charism, for that is their source: promotion of fully human life,[24] guided by openness to truth and new understanding, fostered through the indispensable means of life-long, assiduous study; and above all, the very 'essence of Dominican spirituality', seeking to be actively 'present to God' and 'present to the world' with all its new and emerging possibilities.[25]

---

22. Rule & Constitutions-Sisters of St Dominic, Cabra, Dublin 1843, Ch. IX 'Of the Schools', 45–55. HCC Archives.
23. Annals of Cabra Dublin, 1647–1912, 101–104, cited in Gabrielle Kelly, 'By the Light of the Cross: Cabra Dominicans in South Australia—Founding Ideals' in Kelly G & Saunders K, eds., *Towards the Intelligent Use of Liberty—Dominican Approaches in Education* (Adelaide: ATF Theology, 2014), 443–444.
24. Dominic's passionate purpose, preaching/teaching whatever would be 'useful' for the health and flourishing of souls (*salus animarum*), was intentionally identical to that of Jesus, himself the incarnate revelation of God's passionate purpose—*I have come that you may have life, life to the full* (Jn 10:10).
25. Edward Schillebeeckx OP, Dominican Spirituality or The "Counter-Thread" . . . in the Dominican Family Story', www.dominicanwitness.com, 8; also accessible in Erik Borgman, *Dominican Spirituality An Exploration* (London: Continuum, 2001), 92–110.

Success and expansion of the schools

Mother Columba, as both graduate and exemplar of this tradition, widely acknowledged for her own literary culture, broad interests and progressive attitude, was well-equipped to lead re-invigoration of the mission. The first years in Adelaide, though not without success,[26] had been undermined by stress and conflict, but Mother Columba's re-energising presence in 1875 brought new hope. The academic curriculum, as for Cabra Dublin above, was consolidated, with music, drawing, dancing and singing offered as extras. Renewed trust for the future led to more reinforcements, with another five Irish sisters arriving in 1876. More would come later. In addition, over twenty local women joined the community during the next two decades.[27] By 1880, just five years after M Columba's arrival, the Dominican school in Franklin Street was again recognised, as it had been a decade earlier,[28] as having 'already attained a well-deserved reputation as an educational institute'.[29] More was to follow.

By the early 1880s, M Columba and the community, looking ahead to the needs of the growing society around them, and with great trust in Providence, began plans for a second foundation beyond the city centre. This was prompted not only by increasing enrolments but also the need for a more spacious environment for the boarding school. Insecurity of tenure on the Franklin Street property, leased from the diocese at the time, had also been an unsettling economic factor. By 1886, with generous support from benefactors, a new motherhouse, boarding and day school, named Cabra after the mother house in Dublin, was established at Goodwood South in what was then entirely farm land. The area was later renamed Cumberland Park. Existing boarders moved to 'new' Cabra, and both schools, St Mary's, Franklin Street (day school only) and Cabra, continued to offer the now well-established broad academic curriculum. [Unrecognised at the time, these developments were taking place in the context of continuing Aboriginal dispossession. See Appendix below.]

---

26. See footnote 13 above.
27. Northey, *Living the Truth . . .*, 84.
28. See footnote 13 above.
29. The *Advertiser*, reprinted in the *Catholic Record*, 6 February 1880. James, S (ed) 'The History of St Mary's College, Franklin Street, 1869–1986', 1985, 3, cited in Kelly, 'The Dominican Sisters' Contribution to Education for Girls in Early SA', 1989, 25.

The move to 'new Cabra' in the countryside was not the only response to needs of the emerging future. Another significant development in South Australia, with repercussions for the sisters' educational mission, was the establishment of the University of Adelaide in 1876.[30] It was consistent with the Cabra Dublin tradition that the sisters would take advantage of any expanding opportunities for their students. Hence, when the University instituted Preliminary, Junior and Senior public examinations for schools from 1887, Mother Columba's policy, against the grain of some parental and episcopal reluctance, ensured the curricula at both Cabra and St Mary's were adjusted to prepare students for those examinations.[31] They were among the first girls' schools—if not *the* first[32]—in Adelaide to do so. In the next decade, students from both schools continued to achieve creditable performances in those examinations, with one student obtaining first place in Junior Mathematics in 1889.[33] Though the sisters generally subscribed to the prevailing view of women's place in society, recognising that most of their students too were destined to be 'mothers of the nation'[34], they did not agree that public examinations were unnecessary for girls, or would 'unfit them' for their role.[35] With Mother Columba's—and the sisters'—unwavering advocacy for longer school attendance, and support for academic studies and public examinations for girls, the sisters held open for their students the possibility of wider horizons. A former Franklin Street scholar was just such a trail-blazer in this regard: Blanche McNamara, in 1897, was the first woman appointed an inspector of schools in the Education Department of South Australia. Not long afterwards, Alice Grant Rosman, an old scholar of both St Mary's and Cabra, went to England in 1911 where she became a successful author of popular fiction. At the same time, in recognition of realities, the curriculum was also

---

30. Women studied alongside men from the beginning in 1876; by 1881 they were admitted on equal terms.
31. Northey, *Living the Truth* . . ., 117; Kelly, 'The Dominican Sisters' Contribution . . .', 30–32.
32. Holy Cross Congregation Archives—Obituary, M Columba Boylan.
33. Kelly, 'The Dominican Sisters' Contribution . . .', 24–25; Northey, *Living the Truth* . . ., 118.
34. Alison Mackinnon, 'Educating the Mothers of the Nation' in Bevege et al (eds) *Worth Her Salt: Women at Work in Australia* (Sydney: Hale & Iremonger, 1982).
35. Kelly, 'The Dominican Sisters' Contribution', 32; Northey, *Living the Truth* . . ., 118.

adjusted to include domestic arts such as cooking and dressmaking, and commercial subjects—shorthand, typing and book-keeping—for those who would seek employment in the world of work.

Within eleven years of Mother Columba's arrival, two substantial Dominican Convent schools, both offering an academic curriculum, were flourishing in Adelaide. In response to need, three more were founded within the following seventeen years, with generous assistance from benefactors on each occasion. In 1891, the mid-north Kapunda parish priest requested the Dominicans to take over the local school from the Sisters of St Joseph. By 1892, a newly—built convent school, St. Rose's, was opened. In 1899, a fourth foundation was made at suburban Semaphore on the Le Fevre peninsula, where previously there had been no Catholic school. In 1903, also in suburban Adelaide, a fifth foundation was made at Glenelg, where the school was taken over from the Sisters of St Joseph.

Mother Columba's reputation

Throughout these years of expansion, Mother Columba was esteemed not only for her cultured, wise and clear-headed management capacities, but equally for her pastoral gifts—a 'key-note' gentleness, unruffled calm and gift for friendship. Her keen sense of beauty, notably in the magnificence of creation, is poignantly revealed in the diary of the journey to Australia. Also glimpsed there, at the moment when the home-land finally disappeared from sight, is the acute inner sorrow and loss at leaving forever 'all that they most loved and prized'.[36] Mother Columba's pastoral care of the sisters was given particular expression in her practice of accompanying them to each new location and staying with them for several weeks to ensure that both school and community were well-settled and functioning properly.[37] Aware of the educative value of good literature, she was much appreciated too for ensuring the establishment of suitably-stocked libraries in each community and school. Even after encroaching illness incapacitated her, Mother Columba, ever-committed to providing the best for the students, still found time to check the quality of books proposed for

---

36. Journal of the Voyage—From Cabra to Adelaide, 29 October 1874–4 January 1875, 8, 14, 18, 4. HCC Archives.
37. Northey, *Living the Truth* . . ., 93–94.

prize-giving. Apparently, her readiness to advise pupils on literary matters was legend, and it seems she was not averse to employing mild sarcasm on occasion to convey disapproval of suspect topics such as fortune-telling.[38]

What stands out in the memory of those who knew Mother Columba is the priority that motivated her: care for the best interests of the young people. Delivering on the substance of quality education was more important for her than 'brilliant publicity'.[39] In later life, former students remembered her as an accomplished linguist and teacher, gentle and firm, but 'absolutely just';[40] as 'beloved Mother Columba', whose 'gentle and just dealings and kindly interest . . . counted for much with the girls.'[41] Yet another old scholar poetically celebrated her as 'cherished friend' in childhood's hours, and bade her, beyond death, 'be still my friend '![42] Nor did Mother Columba's care for students stop at the end of school days. Aware that humans *do not live by bread alone*,[43] she instituted annual retreats at Cabra for young women in post-school years. While directed in the customary way by the priest engaged for the purpose, Mother Columba, exercising her Dominican mandate to 'proclaim the Word', personally made time to convey words of spiritual wisdom to these young women by reading carefully chosen passages to them from selected books.[44]

Conclusion

By the time of her death on 3 May 1910, Mother Columba had more than carried out the task entrusted to her. Not only had she gently led in picking up pieces from earlier failures and setbacks; she had strengthened foundations at St Mary's and established 'new Cabra' on spacious grounds, a centre of Dominican prayer and learning, oriented to the coming century. Even in small ways, true to the

---

38. 'A Great Educationist', The Late Mother M Columba, eulogy, *Southern Cross*, Adelaide, 13 May 1910.
39. Ibid.
40. Alice Grant Rosman in *Veritas* 1939, 14.
41. Alice O'Driscoll, Dominican Old Scholar, in *Veritas* Jubilee Number, 1886–1946, 28.
42. Adelaide Primrose Gatzemeyer, 'In Memoriam Mother Columba', *Veritas* Golden Jubilee, 1918, 26.
43. Deuteronomy 8:3; Matthew 4:4.
44. 'A Great Educationist', *Southern Cross*, Adelaide, 13 May 1910.

essence of Dominic's *genius*[45]—his *creative contemporaneity*—Mother Columba had responded to new developments by adapting programs inherited from Cabra Dublin to meet the needs of the emerging social and educational environment. 'A most cultured lady, and a scholar in the best sense . . .',[46] she had soundly shaped the first generation of Dominican education in South Australia. 'Her presence has gone but her spirit survives',[47] and in the mysterious communion of saints and elders not far from our presence, she would most certainly 'still be friend' to the learners and educators at St Mary's and Cabra.

References

Erik Borgman, *Dominican Spirituality* (London: Continuum, 2001).

Helen L Northey, *Living the Truth—The Dominican Sisters in South Australia 1868-1958* (Adelaide: Holy Cross Congregation of Dominican Sisters, SA, 1999).

Gabrielle Kelly, 'By the Light of the Cross: Cabra Dominicans in South Australia—Founding Ideals' in G Kelly OP & K Saunders OP, eds., *Towards the Intelligent Use of Liberty: Dominican Approaches in Education* (Adelaide: ATF Theology, 2014), 439–451.

_____ 'The Dominican Sisters' Contribution to Education for Girls in Early South Australia.' M. Ed. course work paper, University of Adelaide, November 1989.

Alison Mackinnon, 'Educating the Mothers of the Nation' in Bevege et al (eds) *Worth Her Salt: Women at Work in Australia* (Sydney: Hale & Iremonger, 1982).

Margaret Press, *From our Broken Toil* (Adelaide: Catholic Archdiocese of Adelaide, 1986).

M-H Vicaire OP, ed. Peter Lobo OP, *The Genius of St Dominic* (Nagpur, India: Dominican Publications, 1990).

Holy Cross Congregation Archives, Adelaide, South Australia:

Annals of Cabra Dublin, 1647–1912; Annals Holy Cross Province, 28;

---

45. Genius: Macquarie Dictionary—'exceptional natural capacity for creative and original conceptions'. Cf M-H Vicaire OP, *The Genius of St Dominic*, ed., Peter Lobo OP (Nagpur, India: Dominican Publications, 1990), 21.
46. Quote from death notice in 'public paper' (not able to be identified)—Boylan papers, notes by M Catherine Kavanagh OP, Holy Cross Congregation Archives.
47. Golden Jubilee 1918 *Veritas*, 11.

Notes for the Annals, 1868-1934-43; Rule and Constitutions, Sisters of St Dominic, Cabra, Dublin 1843;

Journal of the Voyage from Cabra to Adelaide, 29 October 1874—4 January 1875;

Veritas Golden Jubilee, 1868-1918; *Veritas* 1939; *Veritas*, Jubilee Number, 1886-1946.

Boylan papers: 1) Community obituary; 2) 'A Great Educationist', *Southern Cross*, Adelaide, 13 May, 1910, 8.]

Southern Cross & Catholic Herald South Australian Chronicle & Weekly Mail

APPENDIX

Sorry!

This story—newly flourishing educational establishments for the well-being of young people (a 'blessing' for the colony, some were saying) and the celebration of one of *our* tribe's significant elders—must not be told without acknowledging the concurrent dispossession of the Aboriginal inhabitants. Even before actual settlement of the South Australian colony, the Kaurna people of the Adelaide Plains and their neighbours on Fleurieu Peninsula, the Ramindjeri, had been severely impacted by smallpox or chickenpox epidemics via River Murray traffic from New South Wales. It is believed the Kaurna may have numbered several thousand before European settlement on the east coast, a number which had already dropped to around 700 by 1836. By 1860, increasing settlement and the activities of sealers and whalers in the area had resulted in complete disintegration of the entire fabric of Aboriginal life in the Adelaide Plains area. Through a combination of lethal European diseases and the disappearance of wild life in settled areas, the Kaurna and Ramindjeri were reduced to a 'remnant that merged with other groups, largely losing separate identities'. Hastening the process were the untimely deaths of Elders, the holders of spiritual heritage, thereby further 'eroding clan cohesion'.[48]

This sad transformation had been largely completed almost a decade before the Cabra Dublin sisters arrived in Adelaide, though

---

48. Christine Lockwood, 'Early Encounters on the Adelaide Plains and Encounter Bay' in Peggy Brock and Tom Gara, eds., *Colonialism and its Aftermath—A history of Aboriginal South Australia* (Mile End: Wakefield Press, 2017), 65–66.

its damaging aftermath long continued. Were they—and many of the colonial community of which they became part—aware of this terrible contradiction: that while they were bringing a rich educational heritage for the well-being of young settler people, their collective presence was causing ruination and loss of the life-giving ancient heritage of those other young people and their Elders?

For the suffering and loss of the Kaurna and Ramindjeri people, past, present and emerging, we are sorry![49] It is hoped that the promise of one of the most fundamental convictions of the broad Christian heritage—that heritage rooted in the boundless mercy and compassion of the One Divine Source in Whom all exist—will soon come to greater fruition; that is, the hope that genuine reconciliation, already under way in significant national movements, may bring possibilities for life and well-being for *everyone* in this land, in even greater abundance than in before.

---

49. Dominican Sisters of Holy Cross Congregation, Adelaide, are one in lamenting the Indigenous dispossession and suffering caused by white settlement in these lands of South Australia and elsewhere.

Homily for the funeral mass of Brother Nicolas-Jean Séd Paris, Convent of the Annunciation, October 14, 2022

Eric T. de Clermont-Tonnerre, o.p.

1 Corinthians 15:12–20
Psalm 121
John 20:19–29

It is at the age of 11 that 'Little Nicolas' during a camp and a mountain hike, 'messed up' his leg. After a very delicate operation for a growing young boy, he spent many months in an establishment run by Dominican sisters—he did not know it at the time: it was premonitory, amidst other children. This experience of suffering, forced communal living, disability, and mutual support marked his entire life and later characterized his difficult and painful journey for years. A rare sensitivity developed, delicate on the surface and at the same time very profound, so much so that throughout his adult life, he cared for the sick, both at the beginning of his Dominican and priestly life at Rangueil Hospital in Toulouse, and in recent years as a chaplain at the EHPAD Catherine Labouré.

Everyone who met him and entered into lasting relationships with him was struck by the sensitivity that developed in him, giving rise to great qualities of hospitality and listening. He showed a keen attention to the questions and needs of others, especially towards those who were suffering or going through trials. I know that many of us here have benefited from his listening, his delicacy, his advice, and his support.

In reality, an astonishing capacity for friendship and active friendship characterized Nicolas-Jean. This capacity for friendship was not only natural; it was for him a true spirituality, a life project based on Christ Jesus, the friend of humanity, and on the experience of resurrection, conceived not only as a gift from God to mortal and sinful humanity but above all as a mutual responsibility.

It was the Gospel of Easter evening that inspired this conviction in him. The race of the women and that of Peter and John in the early morning, and the apostles' confinement on the evening of the first day of the week, and also the eighth day—the apostles, in the absence of Thomas, were then ten, the number required in Jewish tradition for the prayer of the bereaved (the Kaddish)—all this expressed the wounded and fearful friendship that the Risen One comes to revitalize by his presence. For Nicolas-Jean, resurrection was not only an announcement, a narrative, a dogma, but also, as he often preached, the main Christian practice. He thought of friendship and lived it as a grace but also as a faithful duty so that the power of resurrection could dwell in our lives, relationships, and communities. Resurrection as the source and fruit of the miracle of friendship. I still remember the phrase he commented on, "If the dead do not rise (emphasizing the present), then Christ has not risen either."

For thirty years, Brother Nicolas-Jean Séd put all the resources of this sensitivity and generosity at the service of Editions du Cerf: his personality, intelligence, analytical and prospective capabilities, skills acquired methodically, little by little, in all aspects of the multiple professions of publishing. He was a knowledgeable and appreciated interlocutor for authors, publishers, and publishing professionals, always attentive to the thoughts and skills of each, but often bringing new perspectives, encouraging to go deeper and farther.

He had immersed himself in publishing long before joining the Dominicans, at the age of seventeen or eighteen, working on the *Sources chrétiennes*. Naturally and simply, in 1981, a year after his priestly ordination, at the initiative of Father Kopf, who had been the provincial prior of the Province of France and then of the Province of Toulouse and who knew him well, he arrived at Editions du Cerf.

Very quickly, he initiated numerous editorial projects and created new collections. Some projects directly served the Church, its theological work, liturgy, and the life and Christian spirituality. Others aimed to highlight the theological and spiritual heritage of other Christian denominations, especially Orthodoxy and Judaism.

His Eastern European Jewish roots, which strongly influenced his sensitivity and thinking, facilitated these relationships. Some collections created by him (Cerf-Histoire, Passages, Patrimoines) aimed, among other things, to bring religious sciences closer to the French University and thus contribute to the influence of French religious publishing at the national and international levels.

In all of this, one can emphasize everything he contributed to the Church in France and to ecumenism during these thirty years, always with:

- A search for God and truth within a broad openness to all men and women of faith, regardless of their background,
- A sense of tradition and institutions when they are a source of responsibility and communion,
- A sense of freedom, marked by the courage of speech, in the face of bureaucratic language and institutional closures,
- A very keen interest in professions, professional skills, and learning

All of this will one day be brought into greater light. However, Brother Nicolas-Jean, the faithful friend of many, the publishing professional, and the great servant of the Church, was, above all for us, a brother and a preacher.

These years at Le Cerf and the last ten years in the shadows somewhat overshadow the Dominican engaged in the life of our Province that he was and with whom we collaborated: prior for six years, definitory, and then a member of the Provincial Council from 1992 to 1997. He was a brother well-acquainted with the province, very astute in his analyses, viewpoints, and advice.

His Dominican life, from beginning to end, was marked by strong friendships and companionships, for example, with Brother Jean-René Bouchet from whom he inherited a good knowledge of our father Saint Dominic, or with Father Kim-en-Joong, whom he faithfully supported for years in his artistic work and the radiance of his work.

Preaching at the Saint-Jacques convent on the feast day of Saint Dominic, May 24, 2012, Brother Nicolas-Jean developed his sermon on Dominican life around three words: truth, mercy, and preaching. And I quote him a bit extensively to conclude:

'To these three words, in the manner of ancient rhetoric, I will add a fourth, and it is not about comedy or satire: Dominican family. Although 'Dominican family' has a beautiful tradition—think of Catherine of Siena and her "famiglia"—I sometimes hear that the word family is not satisfactory, because it is too saturated. I do not propose, with a bit of humour, the beautiful word 'company,' as it is very much in demand: the austere company of pastors in Geneva, our Jesuit friends, the French Academy, and the Republican Guard. I propose—reassure yourselves, it will not be adopted—the word "Dominican school".

In this school, a master is there waiting for us; he invites us in a paradoxical way: 'Come to me, all you who are weary and burdened, and I will give you rest. Take my yoke upon you and learn from me, for I am gentle and humble in heart, and you will find rest for your souls.

In this school, the disciple is not in front of the master, nor is he only following him. In this school, the disciple is beside the master because the yoke is borne together, in a brotherly side-by-side. In the daily routine and trials, this brotherly side-by-side is a messianic side-by-side.'

Brother Nicolas-Jean, we have been happy to live with you for a time, a long time, this brotherly side-by-side, a sign and germ of the Kingdom, and to have worked together for truth, mercy, and preaching, as humble brothers preachers.

The Architecture or Arrangement of the Psalter: A Proposal

Mark O'Brien OP

An initial indication that the 150 Psalms of the Psalter may be arranged in some way is its division into five books. Was this done to form a parallel to, or a link with, the Torah or Pentateuch, which is also divided into five books? Another pointer to links between psalms is that quite a number have superscriptions or titles that attribute authorship to, or associate them with, a particular figure such as 'David', 'Asaph' etc. Some superscriptions include reference to particular events; for example, Psalm 3 has 'A Psalm of David when he fled from his son Absalom'.[1] As well there are superscriptions that name the music to which a psalm is meant to be sung, or an action to which a psalm or a collection of psalms is linked. For example, Psalms 120–134 all bear the superscription 'songs of ascents' and this is generally taken to mean they form a collection of songs for those making pilgrimage to Jerusalem. According to biblical thinking, one always ascends or goes up to Jerusalem and its temple. A question that arises from this evidence is whether the Psalter is what we would call a series of 'loose' collections without any order or purpose, or whether there is some overall order and purpose. For example, are the 'songs of ascents' a kind of handbook for those making the pilgrimage to Jerusalem (in Israelite thinking one always 'goes up/ascends' to Jerusalem from wherever one commences the journey) What might be their function within book 5 of the Psalter and/or within the five books of the Psalter?

---

1. The numbering of psalms in this paper follows the Hebrew/MT and NRSV which differs by a psalm (from 9 to 147) from the Greek/LXX and Latin numbering

Some of the five books seem to share collections; for example the psalms of the 'Sons of Korah' occur in books 2 and 3. Other books however do not have these collections, as for example in books 4 and 5. This raises the question whether the books were assembled somewhat independently of one another and may have been in circulation and use for some time before being linked together to form five books of the Book of the Psalter. If this were the case the order of the psalms was probably well established and not altered when the Psalter was finalised. It is generally accepted that each book ends with a doxology or short song of praise. Were these added later when the once independent books became part of the Psalter? Alternatively, was the assembling and arranging of psalms and collections into the five books, along with the concluding doxologies, an integral part of the formation of the book of the Psalter? On this understanding the psalms may have been arranged or re-arranged to some extent to 'fit' the larger Psalter and its purpose, and the doxologies were an integral part of this process. On this understanding the 150 psalms combine in one or more ways to form a whole that is greater than the sum of its parts. In relation to this it is worth noting some commentators argue that at an earlier stage the Psalter may have comprised 119 psalms in five books, with the long Torah psalm 119 serving as the conclusion as well as forming an inclusion with psalm 1. At this stage, not only did the five books evoke the Torah or Pentateuch, but also the first and last psalm.

An additional factor that has provided grist to the mill of Psalter analysis is the form-critical classification of psalms according to genre or type and the attempt to recover as accurately as possible their original life setting in Israelite society (e.g., as part of the temple liturgy, or as private prayer). This has enabled scholars to better discern the similarity or difference between individual psalms, and this in turn has intensified the question whether, and if so how, the psalms and the five books of psalms combine to produce the larger whole that is the Psalter.

A Way of Reading the Psalter (cf. Architecture or Arrangement of the Psalter)

In an attempt to answer this question I will draw on the information that the Psalter itself provides, such as the five books and the superscriptions, as well as the work of form-critical and other areas of modern biblical research. In regard to the latter, my presentation owes much to a recent publication by Hendrik Koorevaar.[2] Like any literary form, book or library of books, the Psalter is limited. Even though we believe it is the Word of God it is expressed in human words—of a particular language of a particular people and so limited (cf. the remark at the end of John's Gospel 21:24-25). An indication of this is that it seems to select or focus on the period of Israel's story or history from the early days of the Davidic monarchy until the post-Babylonian exilic period when Israel was not able to re-establish the monarchy in its pre-exilic form. We know from the larger HB/OT however that this did not kill faith in the monarchy; instead it fueled hope in a wonderful new era to come in God's good time, one that would be ruled over by the perfect king or messiah. This is indicated by:

- the way the superscription for Psalm 3 refers to an early crisis in the reign of David (his conflict with Absalom),
- the way Psalm 89 at the end of book 3 laments the demise of the Davidic Dynasty at the exile,
- the way book 4 commences with a psalm of Moses (90) rather than David, a kind of return to the founder,
- the way the penultimate stage of book 5 'returns' to the notion of kingship via a Davidic collection in 138-145, but as lead-in to the final series devoted to the praise of God, the Universal King (146-150).
- the fact that the majority of what have been classified as lament psalms are in the first three books, whereas the majority of thanksgiving and praise psalms are in books four and five. This implies that as long as believers stay loyal to God through thick and thin they will eventually win the battle against evil and enjoy blessing. This battle involves the life of each individual whether small or great (king), the life or story of Israel as God's people, and indeed the whole of creation (cf. Genesis 1-3).

The large number of psalms attributed to or associated with David may have a historical basis in that David was apparently a great musician (Saul's lyre player in 1 Samuel 16 and according to 2 Sam 23:1, the 'sweet psalmist of Israel'—ESV translation). Whatever the case it would seem that biblical tradition saw the David psalms as a

---

2. Cf. Hrndrik Koorevaar, 'The Psalter as a Structured Theological Story With the Aid of Subscripts and Superscripts,' in *The Composition of the Book of Psalms* (ed. E. Zenger, BETL 238; Peeters: Leuven, 2010) 579-92.

vehicle not only for portraying key moments in Israel's history but also as prayers that could be invoked by the general populace, both individually and as community. In this way they could also be linked to other collections associated with other non-royal figures such as Asaph and Korah (members of the priestly tribe of Levi), and with other key moments in the people's lives; for example the 'songs of ascents' for those on pilgrimage to Jerusalem.

One can suggest that those who assembled the Psalter placed the 'story' of David and his Dynasty within the larger 'picture' of God's purpose in establishing the monarchy by making Psalm 2 the first royal psalm. It has no Davidic superscription and does not name the king. Hence it can prefigure or serve as a distant prelude to psalms 138–145 which move from affliction and threat to the king and his prayer to God, to thanksgiving and praise of God (144–145). Similarly, the view that the psalms of, or about, David refer also to the people as a whole and God's purpose for them gains support by the way the first psalm of the Psalter speaks of 'the human being' (ha'adam) and God's protection of, and blessing for, the one who is loyal to the Torah (v. 2 'law'). An important link between king and people that makes them effectively one is—Torah. All are called to obey the Torah which, in the context of Psalm 1 probably refers to the whole Pentateuch (called 'Torah' in Hebrew). A key psalm in book 5 is 119, an extended celebration of God's Torah.

Comments on Arrangement of each Book and its Significance for the Arrangement of the Psalter

Book 1 (Psalms 1–41). Koorevaar identifies 4 distinct David collections after the introductory psalms 1 and 2, and proposes that what is commonly regarded as a Torah psalm in no. 19 forms the centre of book 1. A closer analysis leads to the interesting proposal or interpretation that three of these David collections are arranged more or less in a concentric or A–B–A' form, a common one in biblical literature.

- The proposed arrangement of the first is psalms 3–7 (A), 8 (B), 9–14 (A');
- of the second 15–18 (A), 19 (B and centre of book), 20–24 (A');
- of the third 35–37 (A), 38 (B), 39–41 (A').

These proposed concentric or chiastic structures imply that the framing sections A and A' in each collection relate to each other in some way as well as to the central psalm (B in each).

This is perhaps best illustrated in book 1 by taking the second David collection or section of the book, namely psalms 15–24. Hans Winfried Jüngling identifies the following more detailed concentric or chiastic arrangement:[3]

Entrance song	Psalm 15
Song of Confidence	Psalm 16
Song of Lament	Psalm 17
Royal Psalm	Psalm 18
Hymn to God's Glory and *torah*	Psalm 19 (centre)
Royal Psalm	Psalms 20 and 21
Song of Lament	Psalm 22
Song of Confidence	Psalm 23
Entrance Song	Psalm 24

While this may look too neat a structure to some and not respect sufficiently the individuality of each psalm, it does help one to read the collection through and reflect on the likely connection between the individual psalms and whether there is an overall movement of thought and prayer. It is commonly accepted by form critics that psalms 15 and 24 are 'entrance liturgies/songs' and this suggests the collection may be meant to evoke a liturgical encounter with God or that it reflects an actual liturgy.

So after **psalm 15** declares who is worthy to be admitted to God's holy dwelling on earth, **psalm 16** identifies such a person—one who is completely loyal to God. The model here is the Davidic king who openly and honestly presents his struggles to God in the lament **psalm 17**. But God is the one who delivers from troubles, as God delivered David from Absalom (cf. superscription to psalm 3), and this needs to be emphasized and celebrated in the liturgy, and so in the long **psalm 18** the king tells of the victory he gained over oppressors through God's powerful help. While some of the sentiments in this psalm may not be the kind of ones that we would like to pray or

---

3. Hans-Winfried Jüngling, *The International Bible Commentary. A Catholic and Ecumenical Commentary for the Twenty-First Century* (ed. William R. Farmer; Collegeville: The Liturgical Press, 1998), 793.

invoke, claims of utterly destroying one's enemies were a fairly common feature of ANE royal propaganda—and prayer. Liturgies, particularly those designed to boost the morale of king and army going to war, would contain hostile taunt songs against the enemy beforehand and equally hostile victory songs in the event of success in war. A modern parallel would be the taunt songs or anthems of rival footy teams. And because it was believed that victory was given to the king by God, it had to be portrayed as complete, otherwise God was not doing his job of wiping out evil.

The centerpiece **psalm 19** is a hymn that celebrates the greatest gift that God has bestowed on Israel, and is far greater than any victory over the enemy. This is the *Torah*, and at the canonical level of the HB/OT refers to the Pentateuch. It is wrong to think of Torah only in legalistic terms. As already remarked, Torah can mean a law, a law code, instruction/catechesis, and revelation. And God, the master Teacher, knows the best way to teach humans what they need to know and that is to do so via a story. So the Torah is above all the story of humanity and Israel from the beginnings to the edge of the promised land. The story is continued in the so-called 'Historical Books' of Joshua–Judges–Samuel–Kings ('Former Prophets' in Hebrew canon). According to psalm 19, the Torah is for Israel and humanity like the light of the sun that courses through the sky.

Psalms 20 and 21 parallel 18 by giving the prayer of the Davidic king before battle and thanksgiving for victory after battle. Victory or relief from a trying situation does not spell the end of trouble as such and so the well-known **psalm 22** parallels the preceding lament psalm 17, but note how it ends with thanksgiving for deliverance (vv. 23–32). This leads nicely into the following psalm of confidence (**psalm 23**, *the Lord is my shepherd*), which also parallels the earlier psalm of confidence in psalm 16. This liturgical journey or ritual is completed with another liturgical 'entrance song' in **psalm 24**. This clearly echoes the question in psalm sss15 as to who is worthy to enter into God's presence (cf. vv. 3–6) but the focus here shifts from the king (or the one praying these psalms) to God himself who now, in the ritual, 'enters' the ancient gates of the sanctuary as universal and everlasting King.

Book 2 (Psalms 42–72). This book is made up of a collection of Korahite psalms ('sons of Korah') in 42–49 (except for 43), and of Davidic psalms in 51–65 and 68–71. Psalm 72 is attributed to

David's successor Solomon, and psalms 43; 66 and 67 do not have any superscription or ascription. Psalm 43 is often treated as an extension or continuation of 42; note how 42:5, 11 and 43:5 are the same. According to Koorevaar's 'Architecture' the centre of this book is psalm 50, a psalm of Asaph. What is also significant about book 2 is that its psalms generally, though not exclusively, use the general term *'elohim* (God) rather than *yhwh* (Lord). This usage in fact extends to psalm 83 in book 3 and has led to psalms 42–83 being referred to as 'The Elohistic Psalter'. This is further evidence of the varied origins and background of the psalms in the Psalter.

The book commences with two (or one) individual laments and a community lament (**psalms 42–44**). This is a contrast to the way book 1 concludes and in a sense marks a 'return' to the troubled situation voiced in the early psalms of book 1 (cf. psalms 3–7). But one thing that can bring joy to any individual and community in pain is a wedding and so these three introductory laments are appropriately followed by a psalm that celebrates a royal wedding in **psalm 45**, and the promise of descendants. This is surely a sign of God's commitment to all Israel. A royal wedding was presumably celebrated in the temple and so it is fitting to have psalm 45 followed by three psalms that celebrate the Jerusalem/Zion temple as 'the holy place where the Most High dwells' (**psalms 46–48**). With God present there, the holy city is a sure defense against all threats. On the basis of this assurance (expressed in the faith proclamation of the psalms), **psalm 49** can declare to 'all you peoples/inhabitants of the world' the wisest way of living; and that is to place complete confidence in the power of God to 'ransom me from death'. This is followed by **psalm 50** of Asaph which summons the earth to witness God, the just judge, judging his people, Israel. The psalm's presentation of God who teaches and judges the right and wrong way of living forms a parallel with psalm 1, the torah psalm that introduces the whole Psalter, and Psalm 19, the centre of book 1. It is appropriate therefore that psalm 50 is the centre of book 2.

The rest of book 2 is comprised of Davidic psalms (**51–72**). One can divide this second part of book 2 into two sections; **51–64**; and **67–72**, with **65–66** in the middle being two more Zion psalms. Hence another example of a concentric or A–B–A' arrangement. What is noteworthy about psalms 51–64 is that most have a superscription that reports a troubled or threatening time in king David's reign (narrative versions are in 1 and 2 Samuel). The psalm that follows the particular superscription portrays David either confessing sin (as in his affair with Bathsheba; psalm 51), or praying to God for deliverance (psalms 54; 55; 60), or expressing confidence that God will deliver (psalms 57; 58; 59).

The two **psalms 65 and 66** play a similar function within this sequence to the preceding ones on Zion in 46–48. Even though form critical classification identifies 65 as a Zion psalm and 66 as a community thanksgiving, both celebrate God's presence in Zion. This provides a refuge for all those 'whom you choose and call to dwell in your courts' (65:4). Note how psalm 64 and the first part of 66 speak of all (us) before the royal figure (presumably David) gives thanks for his own deliverance in 66:15–20 ('God who did not reject my prayer'). **Psalm 67** may be linked with **psalms 65 and 66** because the same justice and care shown to Israel and its king is there for all the nations. Hence, they should, like Israel and its king, join in praising God.

The Davidic psalms that follow in **68–71** do not refer to any instances in David's life. Rather they follow the more general pattern or sequence of initial praise and thanks to God (**68**), followed by a long psalm of prayer to God in times of strife, but end up in giving thanks to God who hears the prayers of the needy (**69**), and in expressing trust in God (**70**). **Psalm 71** can be read as testimony by David 'now that I am old and grey headed' (71:18) that even though God has burdened him with difficulties God has always proved faithful and richly deserving of praise. The final psalm in book 2 (**72**) has the superscription 'of Solomon' and is effectively a prayer for David's successor, that God will enable him to 'judge your people with righteousness, and your poor with justice'. The king is not there for himself but for the people and this psalm provides not only assurance for the Davidic dynasty but also for the people that God is there for them.

One can see that the Psalter thus far follows in a selective way the faith journey/life of king David up to the succession of Solomon. Yet this spiritual journey of David is set within a larger framework of the journey of God's people with their sorrows and joys. One is related to the other; the king is there for the people and the people are meant to honour and show loyalty to the king who is loyal to God. A key focus for both groups is Zion as God's dwelling place on earth, a sure sign of God's commitment to them and the place where they believe they can have recourse to God and be heard. The sure guide in faith for both people and king in their life journeys is of course the Torah; it is presented as the sure 'way' in contrast to the wrong way of the wicked in psalm 1, celebrated as the light that illumines one's life like the sun illumines creation in psalm 19; and is echoed in psalm 50, the centre of book 2.

Book 3 (Psalms 73–89). This book comprises **Psalms 73–83 (Asaph), 84–85, 86 (David), 87–88 (Korah), 89 (Ethan, the Ezrahite**—a musician in the royal court; cf. 1 Kgs 4:31). A number of psalms in the book are also described as maskils (didactic poems). The book commences with what is classified as a wisdom psalm, namely **psalm 73,** that evokes the two ways set out in psalm 1. The psalmist records his temptation to follow the way of the wicked and his realization that God is the only one who can deliver from such temptation and guide one through thick and thin. The challenge to trust God is exemplified in the next **psalm 74** in which the community laments the enemy invasion of the temple and calls on God for deliverance, confessing in vv. 12–17 its faith in God as savior. It is this faith that enables the speakers to appeal to God. **Psalm 75** is a song of thanksgiving and, within the context, can be taken to celebrate deliverance from the situation lamented in psalm 74. **Psalm 76** follows this up with a hymn of praise to the God who so delivers. It concludes with a call to all to acknowledge and serve God honestly and generously (v. 12).

I see a new section of the book commencing in **psalm 77** with the psalmist crying out in trouble to God day and night. Yet he takes a cue from psalm 75 by calling the mind 'the deeds of the Lord' (v. 11) in redeeming 'your people'. **Psalm 78** can be read as a maskil or didactic/instructional poem that takes up this theme of recalling the 'glorious deeds of the Lord' (v. 4) which, according to this psalm, revealed God's plan to establish David as 'the shepherd of his people' and the one who presumably can save Israel from the repeated lapses in loyalty to God that the preceding verses of the psalm recount. This is a teaching on how God established David—in the past. How does the present situation—of those constructing the Psalter and those using it—compare with the past?

Psalm 79 paints a dramatically different picture of what is happening 'now'; namely enemy invasion and defilement of the holy precincts. After the introductory description of the situation the psalm frames a central plea to God not to hold their ancestors' sins against them (vv. 8–9), and with two appeals for deliverance from the enemy oppression (vv. 6–7, 10–13). **Psalm 80** continues this appeal to God for deliverance from enemies and invokes a similar review of God's saving deeds to the ones in psalms 75 and 77 as a motivation or urge to God to do the same in the 'present' situation.

It is difficult to know how far a sequence of psalms developing a theme extends but because **psalms 81; 82 and 83** are also psalms of Asaph, and for other reasons that follow, one can include them in a sequence or section from psalm 80 (which also of course, as indicated above, relates to psalm 79). **Psalm 81** can thus be read as the glad report of God's response to the dire situation(s) described in psalms 79 and 80. **Psalm 82** offers a further divine response with a sharp reminder about the need for justice in society. If one does not read these in sequence with the preceding psalms then they can be read as making a general reply or teaching; namely that the two arenas in which Israel (continually) fails and which brings divine retribution—often in the form of enemy oppression—are the worship of alien gods (cf. 81:9) and social injustice (cf. 82:3–4). These two areas in which one follows or fails to follow the right way reflect the two parts of the Decalogue—devotion to God in the first set of commands and devotion to neighbor in the second. Two sides of the one coin; you can't have one without the other. Cf. Jesus' injunction to love God and your neighbor as yourself.

Psalm 82 ends by implying that this divine judgement applies not only to Israel but 'all the nations'. God is the universal judge. This provides a lead in to **psalm 83** which urges God to pronounce judgement on the nations named because they have formed an alliance to destroy Israel and blot out its name. This alliance is clearly 'against you' (v. 5) who chose Israel; hence even though Israel is a sinner God can surely not let such a direct affront go unanswered. The rest of this psalm is taken up with an extended petition/plea for deliverance.

Psalms 84 and 85 are Korahite and so can be considered together. The first exalts God's holy dwelling place Zion, a day there is better than a thousand elsewhere and those who enter Zion's courts are assured of divine protection. The second reminds God of his forgiveness of Israel's sins in the past and deliverance from their enemies. Surely God will do the same now and so the psalmist waits expectantly for 'what the Lord God has to say' and that it will be peace for his people (85:8). An individual whom the superscription identifies as 'of David' then steps forward in **psalm 86** as one of God's 'poor and needy' and prays for deliverance. This is presumably not David, because we have had the succession to Solomon in Psalm 72. This is a crisis threatening a subsequent member of the dynasty as its founder was threatened (cf. earlier psalms of David) but who is nevertheless confident that his prayer will be answered, as was that of the founder David. According to Koorevaar this psalm is the central piece of book 3. As if in anticipation, his prayer is followed by another little paean of praise of God's dwelling place Zion in **Psalm 87** and the assurance of God's help for each and every one 'born there' (what might this mean?).

But we have no response from God to the king's prayer; instead the book ends with two lament psalms. **Psalm 88** is a didactic poem (maskil) by an 'I' who is not a king but a certain Heman the Ezrahite. Does it perhaps speak for the king? The final one in book 3, **Psalm 89**, is in the end a bitter lament—and accusation or complaint to God—that despite promises made to 'my servant David', 'you have dishonoured his crown in the dust' (v. 39). This psalm would seem to reflect the Babylonian exile. Like psalm 88, it is not spoken by the king but a certain Ethan the Ezrahite. Thus the two psalms are about the dynasty rather than by a member of it, and there is, at this point, no response from God. The reader arrives at the end of this central book of the Psalter with questions unanswered and faith and hope challenged. One reads on into books 4 and 5 in hope of having faith strengthened and questions answered. Brueggemann sees here the depths of *disorientation* after the initial *orientation* of books 1 and 2, but also a prelude to *reorientation* in books 4 and 5.[4]

Book 4 (Psalms 90–106). It is significant that this book commences not with a psalm ascribed to David but to the founding figure Moses (**psalm 90**). In fact Moses is referred to 7 times (a perfect biblical number) in this book; namely in 90 (superscription); 99:6 (with Aaron); 103:7; 105:26; and three times (another perfect biblical number) in the final psalm of the book, 106:16, 23, 32). Moses is mentioned only once elsewhere in the Psalter, in 77:20. Moses can be said to feature at the beginning and end of book 4 and so is a key

---

4. Walter Brueggemann, *Spirituality of the Psalms* (Augsburg: Fortress Press, 2002).

figure in it. Has Moses replaced David or the Davidic dynasty at this point in the Psalter after the testimony of psalm 89? Not quite, because **psalms 101** and **103** are ascribed to David. There are a number of psalms without superscription or ascription; namely **91; 93; 94; 95; 96; 97; 99; 104; 105; and 106**. It is worth noting that **psalm 92** has 'a song for the Sabbath', **psalm 98** has the simple superscription 'a psalm' about which it is difficult to offer a particular comment, and **psalm 100** is a psalm of thanksgiving.

A general scholarly consensus is that **psalms 93** and **95–99** (all without superscription except **98**) are a collection celebrating God (*yhwh*/Lord) as king. Hence, one could say that book 4 is arranged as a general chiastic or A–B–A' structure, with psalms by or about Moses at the beginning and towards the end of the book (so A and A') framing a central section that celebrates the Lord as universal king (so B). At this point it is worth noting the structure proposed by Koorevaar in 'Architecture of the Psalter' and his identification of **psalm 97** as the centre of the book. The two David psalms in **101** and **103** may be meant to indicate that David and the covenant promise to David of an everlasting dynasty that 89 accuses God of renouncing, is in book 4 embraced or incorporated within the Mosaic covenant. That is, the more specific context of David falls within the larger one that goes back to Sinai and indeed to the promises to the ancestors. This reflects the relationship between the Torah (the Mosaic law and covenant) and the story of the Davidic dynasty in Samuel and Kings. The latter exists because of the former, and its mission is to obey and promote the Torah of the former. T7he Davidic king and people serve the God of Moses, as the collection of psalms on the Lord as king testify.

Book 4 commences in **psalm 90** with a prayer by Moses for mercy and forgiveness; Moses being the one who, above all else, even the Davidic king, can intercede with God. **Psalm 91**, without superscription, can be read as a continuation of 90. It commences with a faith declaration that the one who 'abides in the shadow of the Almighty' God will protect and deliver. This could apply to Moses, a Davidic king or any believer. The psalm ends with God endorsing the claim with which the psalm begins. What better to follow this than a psalm of thanksgiving, no. **92**?

There follows the first of the *yhwh*/Lord as king psalms (**93**). Although the following **psalm 94** does not refer to God as king it describes a key function of the divine King and that is as Judge (v. 2). For its part **psalm 95** is similar to the 'entrance liturgies' 15 and 24 in book 1 and is familiar to users of the Breviary for commencing the Liturgy of the Hours. **Psalm 96** invites or summons all 'families of people' to give honour and glory to the divine King, whose grand arrival is then announced or acclaimed in the central **psalm 97**, in terms that recalls the great theophany on Mt. Sinai in the book of Exodus. The following two psalms, **98** and **99** recall **94** by announcing that the Lord is coming to judge the earth (98:9) because 'you love . . . justice and right' (99:4). Even though it is not included in the collection celebrating God as king, **psalm 100** follows on nicely in inviting 'all the earth' to enter God's gates to give thanks and to praise for God's enduring steadfast love and faithfulness (100:5).

As noted, **psalm 101** is a Davidic psalm and its location here may imply that David/the Davidic king or member of the royal family immediately takes up the invitation in **psalms 98** and **99** to praise God's loyalty and justice and to act and rule in accordance with it. **Psalm 102** has the superscription 'a prayer of one afflicted' and could well be meant to be voiced by the afflicted Davidic dynasty in the wake of the exile. But, as the superscription indicates, it is also available to anyone afflicted. It is a lament psalm but note that there is no question 'why' or 'how long' and no accusation against God of rejection or neglect. In the spirit of the preceding psalms, the speaker in this one is confident of God' saving presence in the midst of terrible affliction.

I would judge that **psalm 103 and 104** form a small sequence in that they deal with two key aspects of God's activity as presented in the Bible. One is God as savior or deliverer and this is celebrated in **103**; the other is God as creator and this is celebrated in **104**. In biblical thinking one does not separate salvation from creation because an integral part of God's salvation is to restore creation to its proper order and the human being to its proper nature as God's image and likeness, and to its designated role as God's viceroy over creation (cf. Genesis 1:26–31). The salvation of creation and every element in it is God's grand purpose or plan, and this is why one can or should pray with confidence to God, no matter how deep the affliction—even that of the Babylonian exile and the demise of the Davidic dynasty.

As noted above Moses is mentioned in **105:26** (and Abraham in 104:6) and three times in **106** (vv. 16, 23, 32). This creates a link with the opening psalm **90**. These two psalms not only form a sequence because of the occurrence of Moses but do so also from a thematic point of view in that they both carry out an extensive review of what we call 'salvation history'—of God's saving deeds in Israel's past.

However, whereas **psalm 105** reviews all the good things that the Lord has done on behalf of Israel and humanity from the covenant with Abraham, **psalm 106** reviews the other side of this 'salvation history', namely Israel's frequent acts of disobedience. And as a testimony to the Bible's realism, it includes Moses' failure at the waters of Meribah in this review (vv. 32-33; cf. Numbers 20). Even the great leader himself stumbled and his penalty was to die outside the land—but not before God had shown it to him from Mt. Nebo in a way that nobody ever had or ever would see it (cf. Deut 34:1-4). As God was just and merciful to Moses so God has been just and merciful to all the people whenever 'he heard their cry' (v. 44). The psalm ends with a prayer that God will now do the same by bringing the exiles home so that 'we may give thanks to your holy name'.

Book 5 (Psalms 107-150). This is the largest book in the Psalter and is made up of what are identified as the following groups or collections of psalms.

- The book commences with an untitled psalm (107).
- A small collection of three Psalms of David follows in 108-110.
- Next is a collection of psalms in 111-117 with no superscription but a number of which begin with 'alleluia' (praise the Lord). Note that the numbering and division of the Hebrew version in this collection is different to the Greek/Latin one followed by the Church (cf. Grail psalms). Psalm 118 may be included in this collection because in the LXX and Vulgate version (as Psalm 117) it begins with the call 'alleluia' which, in the Hebrew version, concludes the preceding psalm.
- Then there is the long so-called 'Torah Psalm' 119. It is an acrostic psalm with 22 paragraphs each commencing with a different letter of the Hebrew alphabet. This may be designed to convey a sense of completeness. It is identified as the centre of the book by Koorevaar and others.
- A collection of psalms follows in 120-134 with the superscription 'A song of ascents'. Wherever one is in the world, one always 'goes up' (ascends) to Jerusalem/Mt. Zion. The collection may well have served as a kind of prayerbook for those in the diaspora making pilgrimage to Jerusalem.
- There are three psalms after the 'songs of ascents' that have no superscription; 135, 136, 137, but I would propose that they continue the focus on Jerusalem/Zion and the temple.

- Psalms 138–145 are another collection of psalms 'of David'
- Psalms 146–150 are a collection of alleluia psalms that brings the Psalter to a rousing and celebratory conclusion (note that Hebrew 147 is two psalms in the Grail numbering; 146 and 147). This brings the numbering of the two traditions into alignment for psalms 148–150).

Psalm 107 is like 105 and 106 at the end of book 4 in that it carries out a review of the past, but in this case it is to endorse the claim of 106:44 that 'he regarded their distress whenever he heard their cry'. Psalm 107 testifies to the truth of this four times (vv. 6, 13, 19, 28). These acts of deliverance or mercy by God in turn testify to God's 'steadfast love' (a better translation than the Grail 'love'; vv.1, 8, 15, 21, 31, 43) for which all should give thanks. Books 4 and 5 are thus linked and one could say that 107 continues key declarations of faith in book 4.

In **Psalm 108** (David psalm) an individual, presumably a member of the dynasty, steps forward to testify that indeed 'your love/steadfast love reaches to the heavens' (v. 4). This means that the nations that dominated Israel and Judah at the exile are all under the Lord's sovereignty (vv. 7–9) and in the Lord's good time 'he will trample down our foes'. **Psalm 109** recounts an extensive curse that David's (or a member of the dynasty) enemies have pronounced against him. These may be subjects of the kingdom or former vassal/allied states who 'in return for my love they accuse'. This is the kind of thing that could well have happened in the wake of the exile—the nations play the blame game. The speaker asks God to expose these curses and the accusations embedded in them as false. He can make this prayer because, as in the preceding psalms, he relies on God's steadfast love. **Psalm 110** provides an assurance for the speaker of psalm 109 of divine support. Note that there is an alternative possible reading of v. 4 that goes 'you are a priest forever, a rightful king by my word/edict'.

As noted, **Psalms 111–117** are regarded as a collection of alleluia (hallelujah) psalms because of the way the collection begins and ends. And, as also noted above, I would include **118** in the collection because it commences (in the Greek/Latin version followed by Grail as no. 117) with 'alleluia'. Because of the size of book 5 we can only offer a glance at these psalms here. In **Psalm 111** God is celebrated for what he does, in particular for his own people (**112**). Such a God is to be blessed forever (**113**). According to **114** rivers, mountains, hills and sea testify to the might of God, and in comparison to God all other gods and idols are mere 'work of human hands' (v. 4—following Hebrew numbering for 115). In **115** and **116** an individual now steps forward to declare that he personally experienced the saving God that the preceding psalms celebrate and for this vows complete devotion to God. All the nations are then called or invited in **117** to praise the Lord. **Psalm 118** is an individual psalm of thanksgiving by one who was in a most dire and threatening situation. The nature of his situation suggests he is a/the king. However, in contrast to lament psalms that describe similar situations in books 1–3, there is no cry to God here of 'why' or 'how long'. Rather there is the testimony that no matter how bad things became the Lord delivered him and he was victorious. As v. 22 states 'the stone which the builders rejected has become the corner stone'. One could read this in a messianic sense. As in a number of preceding psalms, the overall purpose of this psalm is to assert that 'his steadfast love endures forever'.

Psalm 119 is the lengthy Torah psalm, divided, as already noted, into 22 strophes or paragraphs by the 22 letters of the alphabet (it is therefore an acrostic psalm). One could almost say that 119 is itself a Psalter of 22 psalms that nevertheless go together to make up one psalm. Is there a clue in this as to how we are meant to read the larger Psalter? This psalm is regarded as the centre of book 5 and one can see why. In it the Torah is acknowledged and celebrated as the key enduring sign and assurance of God's presence and guidance on life's way. There is an echo here of the Torah psalm 1 that commences the Psalter in the notion of the way/path. The Torah is presented as the voice or word of God speaking to the psalmist (any believer). In effect it is a presence of God as the Master Teacher. And, as pointed out earlier, the term Torah is larger than the word we often use to translate it—namely 'law'.

This has led at times to the false impression that the HB/OT is legalistic. Torah does mean a law, or law code, but it also means instruction/catechesis, and the fact that Hebrew tradition refers to the whole Pentateuch as Torah means that it is above all a narrative or story, because the Pentateuch tells a story. And what is a better way for a teacher to instruct his or her pupils than to tell a story and/or to set their instruction within the context of a story to illustrate the points being made. So the Torah or Pentateuch contains law codes which are illustrated and validated in the surrounding narratives and the narrative setting of law texts indicates that they are an integral part of God's overall purpose for humanity and creation—a world of right order, peace and blessing. The Torah is a key sign of God's enduring steadfast love as asserted in psalm 118.

Psalms 120–134 are 'songs of ascents' and, as noted earlier, are most likely a kind of prayer book for those in the diaspora making their pilgrimage to the Jerusalem temple. But this 'handbook' can also be prayed by those making their spiritual journey to God, wherever they live their lives. In fact the two dimensions are probably not meant to be separated. Our journeys over time and place are all part of our overall journey to fullness of life in God's presence. And what better companion or guide to have on one's spiritual journey or an actual pilgrimage journey to Jerusalem than the Torah, in which God speaks directly to the believer and directs him/her/them in the right way rather than the way of sinners (cf. Psalm 1:1 and 128:1). Even though Psalm 134 is the last one to bear the superscription 'A Song of Ascents', I would suggest that **Psalms 135** and **136** can be associated thematically (and spiritually) with the collection.

Notice how **Psalm 134** commences with a call to praise the Lord (alleluia), directed to all those 'who stand in the house of the Lord', and concludes 'from Zion may the Lord be blessed, he who dwells in Jerusalem'. **Psalm 136** provides the key motivation for doing so, 'for his steadfast love endures for ever' and underpins this by recounting God's steadfast love from creation to Israel's deliverance from Egypt, to their journey to the promised land, where Jerusalem is of course the capital and centre. This review of the past follows the basic storyline of the Torah or Pentateuch. For its part **Psalm 137** ('By the waters of Babylon') testifies that the true Israelite can/will never forget Jerusalem and what it symbolises, no matter where he/she is and however dire the situation. The curse at the end follows logically from this; may all those who set out to destroy God's chosen city and temple themselves experience a corresponding destruction (smashing of children on rocks!). This bit is not of course recited or sung in our liturgy but cursing was a standard part of Israelite and ANE ritual. One expressed what one thought was a fitting punishment, but the matter was left up to God.

As noted above, **Psalms 138–145** are a collection of Davidic psalms. Given that Psalm 72 ends with the note in v. 20 that 'The prayers of David the son of Jesse are ended', is one meant to take this collection as referring only to kings after David, or perhaps even to a hoped for restoration of the Davidic monarchy after the exile (cf. Psalm 89)? The collection is linked to the preceding 'songs of ascents' to Jerusalem by the way the speaker declares in **138** that 'I will adore/bow down before your holy temple'. This suggests the goal and focus of the king's vocation/reign is, like every Israelite, to worship the Lord, the Divine King, in the temple. Notice how the final psalm in the collection **145** commences 'I will extol/give you glory, O God my King'. In **Psalm 139** the royal person who is meant to be judge of his people submits himself willingly to the judgement of God, the ultimate judge who knows all about him and everyone. The psalm ends with the speaker asking God to preserve him from 'the wrong path'. **Psalm 140** could be read as an extension of **139** in that it prays for protection from those who plan and do evil; who walk 'wrong paths' (cf. Psalm 1). Note that, unlike preceding royal psalms in books 2 and 3, there is no anguished cry 'why' and no accusation. The psalm ends with the confident assertion that 'the just will praise your name'.

Psalms 142 and 143 are similar in that they both call for help, confident that one's prayer will be heard (142:7; 143:8–9). **Psalm 144** moves from the situation of threat and distress to faith in (final) victory over enemies. Note the emphasis in v. 10 that it is 'you (God) who give kings their victory, who set David your servant free'. As already noted, in the final psalm of this collection, **145**, the glory for victory and deliverance from oppression goes to the Divine King, God. This final David collection envisions some kind of restoration of the monarchy after its demise in the Babylonian exile (as voiced in Psalm 89) but the reign of the earthly king (or any earthly king) is part of a larger agenda—namely the acknowledgement by all that the Lord alone has universal sovereignty.

One could say that the final group of alleluia psalms in **146–150** are appropriately introduced by the conclusion to the preceding psalm **145** 'all flesh will bless his holy name, for ever and ever'. **Psalms 146–150** outline the most fitting way in which this is to done or will be done (according to God's sovereign will). The collection begins with an 'I' singing alleluia in **146**, then a group ('*our* Lord is great') in **147**. Next, Jerusalem is called to praise God in **147:12f (148 in Grail)**; followed by creation and the heavenly host in **148**, and Israel ('children of Zion') in **149**. Finally, 'everything that lives and that breathes is called to praise the Lord in **150** and fittingly, to musical accompaniment.

In concluding this brief survey of the Psalter and the five books of Psalms in it I would offer the following comment from the German scholar Erich Zenger—in the hope that my translation of his German is reasonably accurate: .[5]

Above all the Psalter displays a 'dramatic' horizon that is framed and constituted by Psalms 1–2 and 146–150 and which gives to the sequence of psalms in the Psalter various interconnected lines of expression.

- One is the Psalter as teacher/teaching of divine and human righteousness.
- A second is the Psalter as a presentation of the dramatic journey of Israel, with God at its head in the midst of a chaotic world, reaching its fulfillment in a cosmic song of praise to God.
- A third is the Psalter as a five-part Torah of the royal/messianic David figure ruling over God's kingdom.
- A fourth is the Psalter as a way of prayer from petition and complaint to thanks and praise, in particular in the move from death to life.

Overall the task of exegesis of the psalms is to present the Psalter as a witness of a fervent search for God by both individual and God's people, but also by those from the larger world, and last but not least to also present it as a general prayer book for Jews and Christians

As a final comment, one may relate the arrangement of the Psalter to the story of Jesus, which goes from initial ministry with healing, the proclamation of good news, to growing hostility (cf. books 1 & 2), to his journey to Jerusalem, to his imprisonment and crucifixion with the quote from Ps 22 (cf. book 3 and psalms 88 and 89), to his resurrection and instructions to the disciples (cf. Ps 119) and the story/journey of the fledgling church (cf. books 4 & 5).

Mark A. O'Brien op
St. Dominic's Priory
816 Riversdale Road
Camberwell, Vic 3124

---

5. Cf. Erich Zenger, 'Psalmenexegese *und* Psalterexegese: Eine Forschungsskizze' in *The Composition of the Book of Psalms* (ed. Erich Zenger; BETL 228; Leuven: Peeters, 2010) 17–65. There are a number of chapters in English and French in this book.

Dominican Spirituality: Prophetic Dynamism in a Creative Engagement with the World

Erik Borgman

To republish a booklet on Dominican spirituality after more than two decades is not self-evident. After all, Dominican spirituality is eminently dynamic. Therefore, as a new addition and update, this chapter on Dominican dynamism. Inevitably it bears itself witness to dynamism: the situation in the Church and the world today is very different from what it was twenty-years ago. In a comprehensive, global sense, but also concretely, in my and probably also in your everyday world. The community of Dutch Lay Dominicans, at the cradle of which this booklet was written, now has over sixty members. The people who started it are all over twenty years older by now. This also applies to me: I am now 66, our two daughters have left home and both have a son of their own. But whatever may have changed, I am convinced that Dominican religious life is more important than ever. Both for me, to live in the here and now, and in view of the future of the world and the church.

The mission to shaking up the world

'Religious men and women are prophets', Pope Francis said in an interview right back in 2013, the year of his election:

> A religious must never give up prophecy [...] Being prophets may sometimes imply making waves. I do not know how to put it ... Prophecy makes noise, uproar, some say 'a mess'.[1]

---

1. A Spadaro, 'Interview with Pope Francis', <https://www.vatican.va/content/francesco/en/speeches/2013/september/documents/papa-francesco_20130921_intervista-spadaro.html>.

That religious life would make 'a mess' and that this is a good thing, seems surprising coming from the mouth of the leader of the Roman Catholic Church. However, it fits with the image the Second Vatican Council gave of the religious life. A great diversity of forms of religious life has emerged, the council observed. No one planned this, but it is a good thing, because in this way 'in accordance with the Divine Plan a wonderful variety of religious communities has grown up which has made it easier for the Church to be equipped for every good work and ready for the work of the ministry, the building up of the Body of Christ'.[2]

Yet Pope Francis meant something more than just that religious life arose in response to ever new, not infrequently confusing situations, and that it is therefore not a set of variations on a basic pattern, but represents a broad palette of forms and charismata. In January 2014, Pope Francis delivered a homily at the Gesù, the main Jesuit church in Rome, the religious order to which he himself [is a member] belonged. When published in *L'Osservatore Romano* the homily was entitled: 'The Society of the Restless'. In the homily Pope Francis characterised the Society of Jesus, as the official name of the Jesuit order goes, at what he considered to be its best moments. In this homily, the Pope said, among other things:

> We need to seek God in order to find him, and find him in order to seek him again and always. Only this restlessness gives peace to the heart [. . .] It is the restlessness that prepares us to receive the gift of apostolic fruitfulness. Without restlessness we are sterile.[3]

---

2. Decree *Perfectae caritatis* on the Adaptation and Renewal of the Religious Life (Oct 28, 1965), no. 1. The Dogmatic Constitution on the Church *Lumen Gentium* (21 November 1964) no 43 uses the image of a tree with many branches planted by God. This suggests that religious life diversified from within. *Perfectae Caritatis* better account for the fact that religious life was regularly reshaped altogether, thanks to initiatives that were based on the assessment of the current situation and responded to it.
3. Homily of Pope Francis in the Holy Mass on the Liturgical Memorial of the Most Holy Name of Jesus' at the Gesú (3 January 2014 <https://www.vatican.va/content/francesco/en/homilies/2014/documents/papa-francesco_20140103_omelia-santissimo-nome-gesu.html>.

According to the Pope, religious life is about an inability to be satisfied with the world as it is. This image of religious life is quite different from the serene orderliness that many people in our time imagine it to be. Given the contrast with their own often hectic and chaotic existence, they sometimes find this orderliness attractive—as an idea at least. According to Pope Francis, religious life shares in the turmoil of human life and human history. Not as an adjustment to it, but rather as a sign of dissatisfaction with it: only *this* restlessness gives us peace!

When asked what he expects from people in the religious life, the Pope replied: 'Wake up the world! Be witnesses to a different way of doing things, of acting, of living! It is possible to live differently in this world'.[4] This different way of living is born from restlessness, a restlessness that gives peace.

Breaking with the ways of the world in the midst of the world

Every form of religious life within Christianity understands itself as a way to imitate Jesus. Jesus Himself, according to the Pope, made 'a mess' of things in his life, and religious people follow in his footsteps. According to Pope Francis, Jesus involved Himself in all the peripheries of the world of his time: the areas and communities that do not actually belong, are not allowed to belong, are excluded and are not seen in their individuality. Religious are called to follow him in this, and they must in no way be deterred from this vocation.

In this, the people on the periphery, the 'poor' in various senses of the word—those with few possessions, those with few opportunities, those with little power and with little prestige—are not, according to Pope Francis, first and foremost the ones to be supported from the centre of society and evangelised by the centre of the Church. It is precisely the poor who are the ones who should evangelize the Church, he explains at length in his first major document, the 2013 apostolic exhortation *Evangelii Gaudium*.[5] Later, he underlines it again in what he explicitly says about religious life:

---

4. *Open to God, Open to the World: Pope Francis with Antonio Spadaro*, (London: Bloomsbury, 2008), 1–22, '"Wake Up This World": Conversation of Pope Francis about the Religious Life', quote 3–4.
5. See especially the Apostolic Exhortation *Evangelii Gaudium* on the Proclamation of the Gospel in Today's World (24 November 2013), nos 197–201 <www.rkdocumenten.nl/rkdocs/index.php?mi=600&doc=4984>.

> It is a hermeneutics question: we can only understand reality if we look from the periphery, not if our gaze is placed in the centre, equidistant from everything. To have a real understanding of reality, we must shift from the central position of calm and tranquillity and move ourselves to the peripheral zones.[6]

Going to and engaging with what is marginal and excluded is, according to the Pope, 'the most concrete way of imitating Jesus' and to the extent that they do so, people in the religious life have a key function in the church and are men and women 'who illuminate the future'.[7]

The Pope hopes for renewal of religious life based on this vocation. Going to the periphery means listening to 'the Spirit who opens new horizons and urgently invites [us] to tread new paths, always proceeding with the Gospel as supreme rule and inspired by the courageous creativity of your founders and foundresses'. Thus, in Pope Francis' view, what is decisive for religious life is not first and foremost what is institutionalised and laid down in the rules and constitutions of religious institutes. What is decisive is the creativity to respond to new situations, see new possibilities and thus break new ground. Founders and foundresses of new forms of religious life have par excellence testified to this creativity. Religious women and men today must show themselves heirs of this creativity.[8] In stressing this, the Pope echoes the commitment of the Second Vatican Council, which declared that since 'the ultimate norm of the religious life is the following of Christ set forth in the Gospels', this following should be considered its fundamental rule. The particular forms of religious institution or families in the spirit of their founders or foundresses should be seen as a particular shape of this following.[9]

Pope Francis also echoes developments in the history of the Society of Jesus, which already early on referred to its uniqueness as *nuestro modo de proceder*, our way of proceeding: our approach, our

---

6. *Open to God*, 5.
7. *Open to God*, 6.
8. See 'Address of His Holiness Pope Francis to participants of the plenary of the Congregation of Institutes of Consecrated Life and Societies for Apostolic Life' (27 November 2014). <w2.vatican.va/content/francesco/en/speeches/2014/november/documents/papa-francesco_20141127_plenaria-vita-consacrata.html>.
9. *Perfectae caritatis*, no 2.

method. This expresses that it is not the obedience to fixed rules that is decisive, but the constant discernment and being guided by what presents itself in the concrete circumstances of life as the will of God. In the period following the Second Vatican Council, Pedro Arrupe SJ (1907–1991), Superior General of the Jesuit order from 1965 to 1983 and of great influence on Jorge Bergoglio who became Pope Francis on 19 March 2013, emphatically presented Jesus in his poverty and humiliation as the example and embodiment of the 'way forward' for the Jesuits.

In this approach, I think, Pope Francis sheds also new light on the Dominican spirituality. In his uncompromising imitation of Jesus Ignatius of Loyola (1491–1556), the founder of the Jesuit order, followed in the footsteps of the medieval movement that had rediscovered the poor Christ with no place to lay his head (*cf* Matt 8:20; Lk 9:56). Francis of Assisi (1181/2–1226), as Ignatius did later on, broke away from his rich and influential milieu, associated himself with the periphery of the poor and deformed lepers and became a beggar, depending on alms. Dominic of Caleruega (1170–1221) left the comfortably regulated life of a Canon to follow Jesus and his apostles in preaching without money or purse, without a travel bag, extra clothes or sandals, as the Gospel phases it. (Matt 10:9–10). The Franciscans and Dominicans opened up a new possibility in the history of the Church and Western culture: to live in the midst of the world in a radical break with the world, in imitation of Jesus who identified Himself with the periphery. With these mendicant orders, faith in God's grace takes the form of a willingness to become totally dependent on that grace. In the midst of contemporary society, they thus embody the question of what is to be seen and heard, said and done, and from what we can live in God's name and in God's light.

Striving to act as if God existed

In 1994, a synod of bishops on religious life and its place in the Church and the world took place under the leadership of Pope John Paul II. In the final document of this synod, entitled *Vita Consecrata,* the John Paul II refers to Mary Magdalene anointing Jesus' feet. He writes that the love for and that the service to people that takes shape in religious life, and which is the response to and expresses gratitude for God's boundless love that is given freely, spreads a fragrance that fills the whole house (*cf* Jn 12:3). 'The house' in this document is mainly seen as referring to the Church as the house of God.¹⁰ Pope Francis sees the periphery not so much as the place where religious should bring the message of the Jesus the Anointed One (the Christ) on behalf of the Church, but as the place where Jesus can be met par excellence. He makes it clear that the spirit of the Beatitudes that religious have traditionally been expected to embody—blessed the poor, blessed the hungry, blessed those who mourn (Matt 5:3-12; Lk 6:20-23)—is the spirit of dependence on God's grace, of vulnerability that knows itself to be dependent on God's love in everything and therefore makes itself unreservedly dependent on this love. This spirit connects with those who have to make 'a mess' of things, because they experience at first hand that the prevailing order in decisive points does not promote but frustrates the good life as it will blossom fully in the kingdom of heaven. This union spreads a fragrance that fills not only the whole house of the church, but the whole house of the world.

In this, I recognise a fundamental insight that lies at the heart of the Dominican tradition and that resonates strongly with me as both a theologian and a lay person. When they preached against the Cathars in southern France at the behest of the pope, Dominic and his Bishop, Diego of Osma, came to realise that the lack of success of customary ecclesiastical action against them was linked to the appeal to Jesus Christ as powerful king. The charge against alleged heretics was that their opposition to this king was illegitimate and that therefore they should submit themselves. Preaching thus amounted to intimidation rather than proclamation. Diego and Dominicus realised that this could not be the way it was meant to be. They started to travel in poverty. To Dominic would eventually be attributed the desire to live like the heretics and preach like the Catholics. The heretics, the Cathars, lived without possession of what people were willing to give them. This is what gave them credibility and credit.

In their own view, the Cathars distanced themselves from the physical existence, which they saw as a form of imprisonment, in order to be able to concentrate on the spirit freed from the ties to this world as much as possible. Dominic, however, saw living in poverty

---

10. Postsynodal Apostolic Exhortation *Vita Consecrata* on Consecrated Life and Its Mission in the Church and the World (25 March 1996), no 104 <https://www.vatican.va/content/john-paul-ii/en/apost_exhortations/documents/hf_jp-ii_exh_25031996_vita-consecrata.html>.

as a form of solidarity, a sign of willingness to live himself totally on the Gospel that he and his followers proclaimed. He read this back in the Gospel of Matthew:

> Take no gold, or silver, or copper in your belts, no bag for your journey, or two tunics, or sandals, or a staff, for laborers deserve their food. You received without payment; give without payment (Matt 10:9–10:8).

Among the established clergy, including the established religious orders, there was much opposition against taking these exhortations seriously. Preachers of Christ wandering around like beggars, sharing in the lives of ordinary people, eating and sleeping in their midst in an inn: in their view it fatally damaged the dignity of the church, of the gospel and of the Son of God Himself. However, it made it possible for Him to be honoured in a new way and in communion with new places and the people tied to them. Specifically, it revealed that—as Pope Benedict XVI and Pope Francis put it in their jointly written encyclical *Lumen Fidei*— that '[t]here is no human experience, no journey of man to God, which cannot be taken up, illumined and purified by' the light of faith in Christ'.[11] We do not have to leave behind what is supposed to be mundane and ordinary for us to connect with God. On the contrary. This insight, which I see strongly present in the approach of Pope Francis in general and to the religious life in particular will eventually hopefully make the canonical distinction between consecrated men and women and lay members of religious families obsolete. It makes clear that there is no principle reason why a married life with all its commitments to the world could not also be a truly consecrated life committed to God.

Lumen Fidei sees the light of faith shining even in people who may not believe, but who are longingly searching:

> To the extent that they are sincerely open to love and set out with whatever light they can find, they are already, even without knowing it, on the path leading to faith. They strive to act as if God existed . . .[12]

---

11. Pope Benedict XVI and Pope Francis, encyclical *Lumen Fidei* (29 June 2013), no 35.
12. Pope Benedict XVI and Pope Francis, encyclical *Lumen Fidei* (29 June 2013), no 35.

This is ultimately what I consider for myself to be the core of the religious life: in the midst of the world of secularisation and many variations of denial of God, to strive to act, think and speak as if God existed, to live in a way that enables the desire for God to show up and is shaped by the prayer that God will fully reveal his existence. From the discovery that a life that does not make space for and pay attention to God is not completely and truly a life.

As I see it, the tradition of religious life makes it clear that a good and truly meaningful life is responding to and enforcing the desire for the God without whom there is ultimately no life. In our longing, our life is linked to the God who awakens the longing and to whose presence it bears witness in this longing. Those who indeed live this way embody in the present the breakthrough of God's future which, as it is written, is "making all things new" (Revelation 21:5). Including the religious life itself.

Constantly reshaping our vocation

This also goes for the religious life and the Dominican life [themselves]. In the so-called Fundamental Constitution that was added to the Dominican Constitutions after the Second Vatican Council, giving a concentrated presentation of the spirit and thrust of all the rules and regulations that follow, this is stated in a somewhat hidden way. It is explained that the Order is governed democratically to ensure 'that the Order's mission is advanced and that the Order itself is suitably renewed' and to stimulate that the ongoing developments are evaluated:

> This constant renewal of the Order is demanded by the Christian spirit of continuing conversion and by the Order's special vocation, which compels it to adapt its presence in the world to the needs of successive generations.[13]

---

13. Quoted in *Liber Constitutionum et Ordinationum Fratrum Ordinis Praedicatorum*, Roma: Convento S. Sabina 2023, *Constitutio Fundamentalis*, § VII. See <https://www.op.org/docs/860/1_lco-book-of-constitutions-and-ordinations-home-doc-en-5fbf8ea66d4ae/1BkPq4DjgvcPJL2ULH-y6ukCyIdKFM7RA/LCO%20 2023%20-%20Versio%20Latina>.

In other words, the Dominican Order has a structure that enables it to continually redefine its place in the world and its current understanding of its mission to evangelise. This is necessary for the Order to remain what it is: 'wholly dedicated to the proclamation of the Word of God'.[14] Indeed, it is its presence in the world that makes this proclamation possible, since it is to this world that the Word is proclaimed and in this world that the Word is to be heard. It is therefore necessary to keep reviewing the actual shape of the Order and, if necessary, to adapt it to changing circumstances.

This implies, I would suggest, that Dominicans are not primarily concerned with the fulfilment in what is in their constitutions and ordinations, not even when this Rule—very sensibly!—prescribes us to celebrate liturgy regularly and thereby make visible, among other things, that our communities constitute ways of being church and live their lives in the light of God's presence. The Book of Wisdom tells us:

> I loved [Wisdom] and sought her from my youth;
> I desired to take her for my bride
> and became enamored of her beauty.
> She glorifies her noble birth by living with God,
> and the Lord of all loves her.
> For she is an initiate in the knowledge of God
> and an associate in his works (Wis 8:2–4).

The Praise the greatness of Wisdom continues for a while, and leads to this:

> Therefore I determined to take her to live with me,
> knowing that she would give me good counsel
> and encouragement in cares and grief (Wis 8:9).

The monastic tradition is full of love lyricism for a good reasons: monks and nuns consider divine Wisdom as the bride or groom of their souls. The monastic life is an attempt to develop a way cohabitation with God's wisdom, to make it possible, to arrange life as it would be if it came to that cohabitation—knowing fully well that this will never be quite the case, because God's wisdom ultimately is unfathomable.

---

14. This is how it is stated in the bull by which Pope Honorius III ordered the bishops to allow the Dominicans to preach in their territory: 'Letter to all Prelates of the Church' (4 February 1221), *Monumenta diplomatica S. Dominici,* edited by VJ Koudelka (Roma: Santa Sabina 1967), 145.

The Dominican tradition, however, has a subtle but essentially different emphasis. At the end of the chapter where wisdom is so exuberantly praised, it reads:

> But I perceived that I would not possess wisdom
> unless God gave her to me—
> and it was a mark of insight to know whose gift she was—
> so I appealed to the Lord and implored him,
> and with my whole heart I said: [. . .]
> Give me the wisdom that sits by your throne,
> and do not reject me from among your children (Wisd 8:21 and 9:4).

Begging and longing for God's wisdom *is* communion with her [?]. The liturgy, singing of the psalms, celebrating the Eucharist, praying the rosary, studying a book or aspects of God's creation and shaping our history as it is included in God's redemption: for Dominicans these things are prayers for wisdom that are sounding thanks to the presence of that wisdom. And that presence is in the midst of us, while creation unfolds itself and history is developed:

> Does not wisdom call
> and understanding raise her voice?
> On the heights, beside the way,
> at the crossroads she takes her stand;
> beside the gates in front of the town,
> at the entrance of the portals she cries out.

Thus says the book of Proverbs (8:1–3).

'People do not light a lamp and put it under the bushel basket', Jesus says, 'rather, they put it on the lampstand, and it gives light to all in the house' (Matt 5:15). The Dominican task is to be a lampstand, awaiting and yearning for the light. Thus we start off as a sign of the light to come and announce it coming. And as it comes and enlightens our situation, we are ready to pass it on and thus to contribute to making the world visible in its shine. We ourselves do not possess it or make it present, except by being open to it. Knowing that we cannot live without it we also know that, insofar as we live, we owe it to this light. Even as it may be hidden in darkness, ultimately 'the darkness did not overtake it' (cf Jn 1:5).

In the realm of God's coming kingdom

According to this view, Dominican identity is hidden in the will not to have a fixed identity, not to know who we are. Christians have often thought they had to answer Jesus' question definitively: 'And you, who do you say that I am?' (Mk 8:29; Matt 16:15; Lk 9:20). Dominicans, by the way they imitate the Son of Man, should first of all embody the *question,* I would suggest. What kind of life is this that He is actually living for us? How is it livable under the circumstances that are ours? In what sense does it fulfil our desire by keeping this desire open at the same time? 'Take [. . .] no bag for your journey, or two tunics, or sandals, or a staff,' says Jesus according to the Gospel of Matthew when he sends out his disciples (Matt 10:10). With the same command, Dominic then also sent out his disciples. '[F]or laborers deserve their food', Jesus motivates this mission. There is no shame in not being able to provide for yourself what you need. You embody something of significance; there is nothing wrong with having to get what you need from others to keep on doing that.

Indeed, you embody something of significance by making visible that in order live it is necessary to receive. That is Dominican identity: embodying dependence, the fact that we are not complacent and complete, that we cannot do it alone. In a remarkable essay on walking, the American writer Henry Thoreau (1817–1862) writes the following intriguing passage:

> I have met with but one or two persons in the course of my life who understood the art of Walking, that is, of taking walks—who had a genius, so to speak, for sauntering, which word is beautifully derived 'from idle people who roved about the country, in the Middle Ages, and asked charity, under pretense of going a la Sainte Terre,' to the Holy Land, till the children exclaimed, 'There goes *a Sainte-Terrer*', a Saunterer, a Holy-Lander. They who never go to the Holy Land in their walks, as they pretend, are indeed mere idlers and vagabonds; but they who do go there are saunterers in the good sense, such as I mean. Some however would derive the word for *sans terre,* without land or a home which, therefore, in the good sense, will mean, having no particular home, but equally at home everywhere [. . .] But I prefer the first, which is indeed the most probable derivation. For every walk is a sort of

crusade, preached by some Peter the Hermit in us, to go forth and reconquer this Holy Land from the hands of the Infidels.[15]

Peter the Hermit or Peter of Amiens (c 1050–1115), in 1095/6, carried out Pope Urban II's call to liberate the Holy Land and, in the process, rallied a large, unruly popular army—which, by the way, was massacred by the Turks after dramatic wanderings and hardships.

What is most remarkable in this passage is that the Holy Land in Thoreau's depiction is not reached by saunterers at the end of their journey. It is conquered by sauntering itself, or rather, it is conjured up by true saunterers being at home nowhere, and therefore at everywhere. Just as an entire area is transformed into a river landscape by the river meandering towards the sea, Thoreau explains. Somewhat similarly, followers of Dominic inhabit the earth as the realm of God by wandering around without possessions, without fixed abodes, without being at home anywhere. By making themselves dependent on it, they awaken the grace and proclaim that people live and can live by it.

To a question from Simon Peter, Jesus says that there is there is no one who has left house or brothers or sisters or mother or father or children or fields for his sake who will not receive a hundredfold now in this age—houses, brothers and sisters, mothers and children, and fields (Mk 10:29–30; *cf* Matt 19:29; Lk 18:29–30). To those who have nothing, everything belongs, and for those to whom this is fully revealed, the kingdom of God is so near is has in fact arrived. For the early Dominicans, the Beatitudes from the Sermon on the Mount were fulfilled, a story from the early days of the Order suggests.

One day, it is said, Dominic sent his brothers out to beg for their breakfast. When they met again, however, they discovered that they have only half of what was needed to feed them all. Dominic burst out into joy, because he and his brothers were embodying the Beatitudes: 'Blessed are you who are hungry now', (Lk 6:21; *cf* Matt 5:6). He danced around and praised God so infectiously that his brothers could not restrain themselves from following his example. A woman passing by took offence at this and questioned: 'Aren't you all religious? Then how come you are so cheerful at this early hour'— apparently she assumed they were drunk:

---

15. *The Portable Thoreau,* edited by C Bode (New York: Penguin Books 1987), 592–630: 'Walking' (1862), here 592–593.

> But when she discovers the real cause of their mirth However, when she discovered the true cause of their joy and saw them rejoicing over their want of food, she was deeply touched, and hurrying home she brought them bread and wine and cheese, saying: 'If you were merry and gave thanks to God because of such a miserable pittance, I want you now to have greater cause for rejoicing'. After this, she withdrew, feeling highly edified, and begged for a remembrance in their prayers.[16]

In this way the second part of the Beatitude comes true also: 'Blessed are you who are hungry now, for you will be filled'. Thus, hunger becomes a first step towards satiation. In this sense, we Dominicans not only live with our hunger, but from our hunger.

---

16. From the so-called *Vitae Fratrum* (1255–1260) on the beginnings of the Dominican order, quoted in P Murray, *The New Wine of Dominican Spirituality: A Drink Called Happiness* (London: Burns & Oats 2006), 59.

Thomas Aquinas and a Vast Universe

Thomas O'Meara OP

The year 2024 is the 750th anniversary of Thomas Aquinas' death. In Naples, Thomas Aquinas after years of lecturing and constant writing and publication (recently commenting on all the letters of St. Paul) had become weak and limited. He would still accept requests to comment on brief texts but could not work on larger projects. At the end of January, 1274, he and companions set out for Lyons and the Ecumenical Council expected to begin in May. Not far north he stumbled on parts of fallen trees and fell. At the Cistercian abbey of Fossanova he stopped to regain his strength but died on March 7.

In 1231 the boy Thomas had been entrusted to the Benedictine monks of the Abbey of Monte Cassino for his education. In 1239, the Norman Emperor in Sicily, Frederick II, directed his armies to expand their occupation of southern Italy. With all the students Thomas was sent home. Someone made the providential but innovative recommendation that he should pursue his studies at the recently founded university in Naples. It was begun by Frederick II in 1224 to rival the new academic center in Bologna. It would reflect the atmosphere of Frederick's court at Palermo where Christian, Muslim and Jewish scholars exchanged ideas and where Arab astronomy and Greek medicine met. Journey can be destiny. This journey of Thomas Aquinas takes him from the rural monastery to the university in the city. It takes him from theology seen as Platonic–Christian spiritual reading and Augustinian paraphrases to theology as the free exploration of faith simulated by Aristotelian sciences. He also entered the recently founded Dominican friars.

In that century of the high Middle Ages the world was changing, expanding. Writings from Arab and Greek worlds held a richer mathematics, medicine, and natural science. Thomas, inspired by his teacher Albert, accepted with enthusiasm that wider world. Albert was a remarkable scholar and teacher, interested not only in philosophy and theology but in the realms of nature. In one of his writings, *De vegetalibus,* Albert created the first extensive presentation of the flora of central Europe. He described more than 350 kinds of plants as well as the basic issues of botany. That spirit of openness Thomas pursued into psychology, theology, and biblical exegesis. William of Tocco was a student of Thomas Aquinas and also his biographer. He observed how the young professor captured the imagination of his hearers by presenting what was new. 'Friar Thomas in his courses stated new problems, discovered new methods, and used new networks of proofs. To hear him teach was to be in contact with a new doctrine supported by new argumentation.'[1] Whether ancient patristic texts or Arab-Muslim compendia Aquinas searched out new resources.

The launching into space of telescopes like the Hubble and the Webb as well as the identification of well over 6000 exoplanets orbiting their own suns have expanded greatly the knowledge of the universe. How would Thomas Aquinas respond to the vastness of this world? Let us look at two topics of today in light of his earlier perspective: the size of the universe, and the likelihood of intelligent creatures on distant planets.

I. Vast Universe

Generally stars are found together in galaxies. The Milky Way is home to more than 100 billion stars. Astronomers had estimated that the observable universe has around a trillion galaxies. However, those estimates are changing because of the power and sensitivity of current telescopes. Quite recent estimates have upped the number of galaxies in the universe from 1 to 2 trillion. By measuring the number and luminosity of observable galaxies, astronomers put current estimates of the total stellar population at roughly 70 billion trillion suns. Nonetheless, they caution that it is possible that there are three times that many stars.

---

1. William of Tocco cited in M-D Chenu, OP, 'Thomas Aquinas, an Innovator in a New World', in Thomas F O'Meara, OP, ed, *Exploring Thomas Aquinas. Essays and Sermons* (Chicago: The New Priory Press, 2017) 1–18.

Aquinas, like Albert, noticed the great variety in Earth's realms of nature, countless kinds of plants and animals, birds and fish. Moved by Aristotle's attention to the activity of beings—from mice to human persons—he emphasised that God is not a static supreme being but an all-active reality. The divine is a being realized in countless activities. 'God is a living fountain, one not diminished in spite of its continuous flow outwards.'[2] Eventually the infinite was motivated to create and sustain other beings. 'God contains existence itself as an infinite and undetermined ocean of reality.'[3] This source causes countless kinds of potential and real beings. The divine motive for creation is unlimited goodness diffusing itself by bestowing existence on others as a creator-artist leads forth beings.[4] Things exist to show God's goodness and to give aspects of it to others. Intelligent creatures are the summit of the universe, existing on Earth and in countless angelic forms. Thomas Aquinas described God as *'maxime liberalis'*— 'generous to the highest degree'.[5]

God intends a universe which is diverse but also coherently arranged. Whatever little we can know about God comes from traces left in creation. 'To the extent that a creature has existence it represents the divine existence and the divine goodness.'[6] The extent of the universe in its enormity is the strongest presentation of God's love and power.

II. Life on the Stars

Tonight, as on every night, powerful instruments of research receiving radio and light waves search out stars far away. However, they are examining stars in a new way. They are looking for planets circling around those stars. Beginning in 1992, planets outside of our solar system have been detected, over 6000 of them. With these celestial objects now called 'exoplanets' Earth has entered into a new world, one that is indeed a vast universe.

---

2. *Super Evangelium Ioannis Lectura* (1:4) (Turin: Marietti, 1952), chapter 1, lect. 3, 20; *Summa theologiae* (*ST*) III, 1, 1.
3. ST I, 13, 11 (Aquinas is citing John Damascene).
4. ST I, 14, 8.
5. '... *maxime liberalis*' (In *Scripta super libros sententiarum magistri Petri Lombardi* 2, d. 3, q. 4, a. 1, ad 3).
6. ST I, 65, 2, 1.

What would Thomas Aquinas say to the likelihood of intelligent creatures living in societies elsewhere among the stars? Are we the only beings in the universe who know and analyse? Does not the countless number of galaxies and suns—and now, planets—suggest that the divine sets forth diversity in intelligent creatures. For Aquinas, creatures' existence hold traces of the reality of God. Intelligent creatures bear the image of God (as mentioned by *Genesis)*, an image found in the ability to know and to be free.[7] Given his emphasis upon higher forms of life is it not likely that the universe hold a number of such peoples.

The Dominican professor affirmed one universe, and he did not think there was life on the planets or stars. He knew that there are some who have posited a number of worlds. Did not those cosmologies locate the origin of the universe in chance and neglect wisdom's order. Aquinas' *Summa theologiae* formally treated the issues of whether 'celestial luminary bodies' were alive. Some Greek philosophers in antiquity like Epicurus and Anaxagoras held that stars were alive and intelligent. Christian theologians in the past differed in their views: Origen and Jerome theoretised about the life and understanding of heavenly bodies while Augustine left the question open. The corporeal serves perception and knowing. However, Aquinas argued, the mineral structure of the moon and planets is not of a dynamic mixture which allows for sensation or intellectual life. Consequently, the lights we see in the sky are not conducive to sensation or intelligent life.[8]

Plural worlds meant for Aquinas worlds of celestial bodies that have no single source or point of reference. He observed that those arguing for a plurality of worlds seem to understand 'world' to be exactly like ours, but another world would be quite diverse from ours. In a commentary on Aristotle's *On the Heavens and the World* Aquinas raised objections against his position of only one world. First, since the power of God is infinite and this one solar world does not place necessary limits upon it, why not think there is another world? He answered that God's power has other goals than fashioning worlds. Second, if other worlds are just like ours they have no purpose; or, if they are different, this world would be incomplete and poorly

---

7. *ST* I, 93, 4 & 5.
8. *ST* I, 70, 3.

conceived. Third, the cosmos is a kind of complete totality, and the goodness of the world's diversity is supported by its unity.[9] What exactly is Aquinas considering? It would seem not to be other units within the one universe, albeit one much greater than the Ptolemaic system of planets and stars, but other totalities, other universes, which have no connection to ours. If he limited intelligent life in our planetary system, still he was open in theory to the possibility of intelligence and grace existing elsewhere.

III. Grace beyond Earth

In light of the contemporary estimate of the number of galaxies and the identification of exoplanets theology can ask further, Do intelligent creatures normally, rarely, or usually draw forth from God's free plan some special contact? What religions call 'revelation' and 'grace' are expressions of a special presence of God. Faith holds that God silently and really touches men and women in a special way. Jesus' 'Kingdom of God' and Paul's 'Life in the Spirit' are words for a special atmosphere existing in human society.

If other planets have peoples with their own psychologies and existentials, such worlds have their own understandings of revelation and grace. 'It is not suitable that God would provide more for creatures being led to a natural good by divine love than for those creatures to whom that love offers a supernatural good.'[10] Aquinas is an advocate of grace. Intelligent extraterrestrials would mean more recipients of graced life. It is unlikely that there are millions of bands on the

---

9. Aquinas, *In Aristotelis De Caelo et Mundo Expositio* (Turin: Marietti, 1952), I, lect. 19, 94. Elsewhere he gave an argument from the centrality of Earth in its gravity. 'For it is not possible for there to be another Earth than this one, because every earth, wherever it might be, would be born by nature to this middle point. And the same reason applies to the other bodies which are parts of the universe' (*ST* I, 47, 3). The former Parisian professor Peter of Spain when elected pope asked the archbishop of Paris Stephen Tempier to look into ideas of various Aristotelian thinkers possibly injurious to the faith. A commission came up with 219 propositions, a few of which were positions of Aquinas. One of those condemned held that there could be only one world (see Jean-Piere Torrell, *Saint Thomas Aquinas* 1 *The Person and His Work* [Washington: Catholic University of America, 1996], 298–301; JF Wippel, 'The Condemnations of 1270 and 1277 at Paris', in *Journal of Medieval and Renaissance Studies* 7 [1977]: 169–201).
10. *ST* I-II, 110, 2.

spectrum of natural life but only one form of created supernatural life, since a spiritual and graced existence is higher and richer. There might be a number of modes of supernatural life with God, a variety of divine life shared with intelligent creatures in a million galaxies. We should not project our species and world onto other planets. Human beings do not honor revelation by projecting terrestrial religion (and its context of proneness to evil and sensuality) beyond Earth.

Incarnation is the human and divine climax of grace. It is the high intensification of salvation-history and of the missions of the Trinity to creatures. Thomas Aquinas made an interesting observation about the incarnation of Trinitarian persons. If he did not entertain the reality of intelligent beings on distant planets, nonetheless, he strongly rejected constrained terrestrial views on what God could or could not do. For a careful thinker like Aquinas the humanity of Jesus of Nazareth remains limited and minute compared to the all-powerful Word of God. 'The power of a divine person is infinite and cannot be limited to anything created.'[11] Could there be other incarnations? Aquinas asked, Could the Trinitarian persons in God be incarnate in creatures other than Jesus of Nazareth? He said, Yes. An incarnation is only one divine activity; it involves one creature as the object of that one special divine relationship. It hardly presents all that God can do and is doing.

> If a divine person could not assume another [created nature], then the personal mode of the divine nature would be enclosed by one human nature. But it is impossible for the Uncreated to be circumscribed by the created. So, it is plain that whether we look at the divine person in regard to its power (which is the principle of the union) or in regard to its personhood (which is the term of the union), it must be said that a divine person, over and beyond the human nature which it has assumed, can assume another distinct intelligent nature.[12]

All three persons could become incarnate because incarnation is one aspect of divine power. The life of Jesus on Earth does not curtail the divine Word's activities.

---

11. ST III, 3, 7.
12. ST III 3, 7.

Incarnation exists to show creatures God's love for them. An incarnation is valuable; a variety of them is perhaps normal and ordinary for the Trinity. Origen held that the persons of the Trinity sought out incarnation; they passed through the spheres of stars and planets often in ways that included incarnation. Each created intelligent creature touched by incarnation would have a similar stance in terms of the presence of a divine person but culturally and religiously have something proper to its world. 'God by assuming flesh does not diminish his majesty; and in consequence did not lessen the reason for reverence toward him which is increased by this further knowledge of him. On the contrary, from the fact that he willed to approach us through the assumption of flesh he attracts us to know more about him.'[13]

+++

Aquinas would be comfortable learning of a wider universe mirroring its Creator even if he has doubts about inhabitants on the planets or stars. His theology in two central points—divine expansion and incarnation potentiality—supports the results of astrophysics today. He was not afraid of the new directions of university and theology in his time, and he might greet the new directions suggested in the century now unfolding.

---

13. ST III, 1, 2, 3. "Christ is the head of all human beings but diversely" (ST III, 8, 3).

New Theological Tendencies[1]

Pietro Parente

The Modernist crisis, at the beginning of this century, brought about a general confusion in the field of the sacred disciplines. A violent attack was set in motion against the traditional scholastic theology which drew its strength from the patronage of St Thomas and of his great commentators. Its prevailingly speculative character was disdained, its syllogistic shape, its method, its abstractedness were subjected to ridicule; a lack of critical understanding, of historical documentation, of exegetical exactitude of the sources were censured in it. Finally, the absence or the suffocation of religious vitality was blamed on scholastic rigidity. The echo of the invectives of Laberthonnière, of Loisy, of Le Roy against scholasticism and especially against Thomism has still not faded.

The Encyclical *Pascendi* scored a direct hit on Modernism; the Successors of Pius X insistently recalled the minds that had lost their way to the secure doctrine of St Thomas. Among Catholic masters, not a few, holding steadily to the traditional positions, prepared themselves to defend them from the modern attacks with criteria and methods that were more in accord with the altered requirements of the times. Thus there grew up new forms and new tendencies in the treatment of the theological problematic which involves divine revelation and thus dogma. But this work on such a delicate subject was at times, and still is, the occasion for scholarly mishaps for anyone who dedicates himself to it, though with good intentions, yet without a vigilant caution.

---

1. Originally published in *l'Osservatore Romano* (9/10 February 1942): 1. Translated by Alessandro Cortesi, OP with revisions by Denis Minns OP.

A painful example of mishaps of this kind is the recent decree of the Holy Office, by which two books which deal with theology, with its natures and principally with its method, were placed on the Index. They are two lively little works, one by Fr Chenu (*Une Ecole de théologie: Le Saulchoir*, 1937) and the other by Fr Charlier (*Essai sur le problème théologique*, 1938), which reveal two minds daringly open to the new methods and the new currents of theological thought, which had their inception under the pressure of Modernism.

No doubt, Chenu and Charlier, two scholars who belong to a well-known cultural group, which glories in the names of Gardeil, of Lemonnyer, of Mandonnet, have written with the best of intentions: but the lively temperament, the love of novelty, a boyish, so to say, audacity of attitude with respect to the traditional systems, have driven them to trace out the lines of a reform in the field of theology which, if if it is not without some good observations and some justifiable emphases, is nevertheless unfortunately infected by some dangerous principles, which lend themselves to real deviation from orthodox doctrine.

The decree of the Holy Office is not a surprise for anyone who has attentively read the two books, with which fault has already been found by weighty theologians, like Boyer and Gagnebet. The two works present a marked mutual affinity, even a substantial communality of ideas and of attitudes. Fr Charlier follows the boldness of certain original theories of Chenu, and goes even further. Both throw discredit on scholastic theology, on its speculative character, on its method, and the worth of the conclusions that it draws from the data of revelation. And the discredit redounds, naturally, also to St Thomas.

When the two writers insist on the merely analogical nature and on the relativity of the dogmatic formulae consecrated by the ecclesiastical Magisterium, when Charlier affirms that true rational demonstrations cannot have a place in theology and that the theologian, rather than reasoning, should contemplate and sense the mystery, inserting himself in the mystical vitality of the Church, one has the impression of finding oneself confronted with a strange disvaluation of human reason in favour of sentiment, of religious experience, that makes one think of the theories of Mohler, later developed and exaggerated by the Modernists.

Chenu and, even more, Charlier bring forward unacceptable ideas on the development of revelation and of dogma. For them, the datum of revelation is not fixed and immoveable, but is in continual growth, not only in the minds of the faithful who come to know it, but also intrinsically, in itself: revelation is, as it were, in act in the living Magisterium of the Church, and it evolves and grows together with the Church. As though it were not true that revelation closed with the death of the last Apostle and was entrusted as a sacred deposit to the ecclesiastical Magisterium, to be guarded faithfully (Vatican Council)! Thus an evolution of dogma that is not only subjective, but also objective, contrary to what the Church teaches in opposition to Modernism (*Encyclical Pascendi*)

There is also to be deplored in these two books the disvaluation of the positive proofs for theological theses from Sacred Scripture and from the Tradition, as also the strange identification of the Tradition (source of revelation) with the living Magisterium of the Church (guardian and interpreter of the divine word).

In short, this *new theology*, of which the two worthy fathers have made themselves the champions, while it rudely attempts to demolish the system long-since classical in our schools, does not present safe subject matter or healthy criteria for a reconstruction that is in harmony with the ineluctable demands of a perfect *orthodoxy*.

Any theologian worthy of that name should not hold rigidly, in fact of method, to the old positions, but can and ought to take into account his context and his time, in order to profit from the good that is to be encountered in the new ideas and in the new directions, with a view to updating his teaching and his researches.

But no new tendency, no critique, no demand of modern thought can ever permit the Catholic theologian to damage or to modify in any way what are the master-lines of the immutable truth revealed by God, guarded, interpreted and defined by the infallible Magisterium of the Church. A healthy spirit of conservation, tempered by an enlightened sense of modernity: but not a bellicose rebellion against the past nor a mania for novelty and progress or a spirit of adventure precisely there where tradition and authority have normative value and right of prevailing over the individual judgement and reasoning.

P Parente

A Brief Note on Parente, Garrigou Lagrange and Chenu

Alessandro Cortesi, OP

In 1942 Pietro Parente was professor of dogmatic theology at the Pontifical Lateran University, in Rome. In 1955, he was appointed Archbishop of Perugia by Pius XII. Four years later, Pope John XXIII appointed him Counsellor of the Congregation of the Holy Office, and he was Secretary of the Congregation from 1965 to 1967.

The Roman theologian, was representative of a theology fixed on the deductive method of conclusions and of neo-scholastic implantation. He was official commentator on the Decree of the Holy Office of 4 February 1942 which put on the 'index' the book of Marie-Dominique Chenu *Une école de théologie* along with the book by PL Charlier, *Essai sur le problème théologique*. Chenu proposed a theology, which took root in the lived faith of the people of God and recalled the importance of experience and history in implementing the theological work. These positions were accused by Parente to be a form of modernism.

On 10 February 1942 Parente wrote an article in *L'Osservatore Romano* that cast strong suspicion on the theology of Chenu and Charlier. The accusation was to discredit scholastic theology, its speculative nature and method and the value of the conclusions it draws from revealed data. Chenu will said that the main accusation made against him was not affirming Saint Thomas as an absolute.[1] The historical approach according to which, on the one hand, it dealt with medieval authors and, on the other, interpreted the challenges of the present was the main problem.

---

1. M-DChenu, A Franco, *La teologia è sapienza. Conversazioni e lettere* (Brescia: Morcelliana, 20180, 150.

At the Second Vatican Council Parente shared the positions of the conservative wing of the *Coetus Internationalis Patrum*. During the debate on the collegiality of the Church, however, he took a surprisingly different position, praising the lines of research of Giuseppe Alberigo, a scholar point of reference for the renewal of ecclesiological thought.[2] When the difficult question of collegiality was discussed, Parente was thus chosen to be the official speaker on the subject of collegiality and showed skills in mediation. In his speech he stated that the recognition of the collegiality of bishops is not at odds with the primacy.

After the Council, Parente, while remaining faithful to the approach of classical scholastic theology, welcomed with moderately positive judgment some instances of Council renewal. He recognised that theology must free itself from abstractness, from detachment, from concrete human problems and dogmatism.[3] In his speech at the beginning of the academic year 1967-1968 at the Urbaniana University he stated that theology builds its discourse on the primacy of the Word of God and on the dynamic conception of revelation and dogma and must avoid 'being a syllogistic system of theoretical formulas'. He showed in such statements that he was a moderate in his view of some of Chenu's writings affirming the historicity of dogmatic formulas and the evolution of dogma.[4]

However, in 1979, considering the *nouvelle théologie* with reference to Daniélou, De Lubac and Congar, Parente once again made a very critical statement that linked the schools of Fourvière and Saulchoir as 'a refermentation of modernism that was affected but not dead'.[5]

Speaking of him, Chenu observed in later years that although he dealt with contemporary theological debates however, he did not have an adequate knowledge of them.[6]

---

2. *Cf* G Alberigo, *Lo sviluppo della dottrina sui poteri nella chiesa universale. Momenti essenziali tra il XVI e il XIX secolo* (Rome: Herder, 1964).
3. *Cf* Pietro Parente, *Itinerario teologico ieri e oggi* (Firenze: Vallecchi, 1968); M Di Ruberto, *Scritti del Cardinal Pietro Parente dal 1933 al 1976* (Rome: Città Nuova, 1976).
4. G Alberigo, *Introduzione* a M-D Chenu, *Le Saulchoir. Una scuola di teologia*, XXIII; J Duquesne, *Un théologien en liberté. J.Duquesne interroge le p. Chenu* (Paris: Le Centurion, 1975), 122-124.
5. P Parente, *Terapia tomistica. Per la problematica moderna da Leone XIII a Paolo VI* (Rome: Logos, 1979), 67.
6. Chenu, Franco, *La teologia è sapienza*, 142.

Garrigou Lagrange had been director of the thesis on contemplation that Marie Dominique Chenu had defended at the Angelicum in 1920. Chenu had a high esteem for his master, but he distanced himself from his theology views and preferred to return to the more lively and fertile 'theological environment' of Le Saulchoir and not stay in Rome after his doctorate. Speaking on Garrigou he wrote: 'He was a man divided in two. On the one hand he was a master of spirituality . . . on the other hand . . . he was too much of Aristotle and not enough of the Gospel and his theology ran the risk of being a sacred metaphysics. It was completely unrelated to the story.'[7]

In 1938 Garrigou took part in a group of Dominican theologians who met with Chenu at the request of the Master of the Order requesting him to sign ten propositions that would remove the suspicions generated by the historical method he had used in his writings. He signed the propositions which were a long way from his perspective but later said that it was had been a profound humiliation for him to do this.[8]

In 1946 Garrigou wrote the article in the *Angelicum* journal in which he took up the expression *nouvelle théologie*, used by Parente four years earlier in reference to the works of Chenu and Charlier, using it to indicate and stigmatise as innovators the approach of the Jesuit school of Lyon, Fourvière, which promoted a theology of return to the sources.[9]

---

7. Duquesne, *Un théologien en liberté*, 38; Chenu, Franco. *La teologia è sapienza*, 30.
8. Chenu, Franco. *La teologia è sapienza*, 32.
9. P Parente, *Nuove tendenze teologiche*, *L'Osservatore* Romano (9/10 Feburary 1942),1: 'In short, this *new theology*, of which the two worthy fathers have made themselves the champions, while it rudely attempts to demolish the system long-since classical in our schools, does not present safe subject matter or healthy criteria for a reconstruction that is in harmony with the ineluctable demands of a perfect *orthodoxy*.' My translation.

Contributors

Erik Borgman OPL, is a Dutch lay Dominican. He is professor of systematic theology at the University of Tilburg, the Netherlands. At the Radboud University Nijmegen, the Netherlands, he was the Director of the Heyendaal Institute, an institute for interdisciplinary research.

Eric T Clermont-Tonnerrre OP, a French Dominican friars has been Provincial of his Province and is at present Prior of one the two Dominican Priories in Paris. He is a writer and preacher and for many years worked at the French Dominican publishing house in France, editions du Cerf, alongside Nicolas Jean Sed OP who died in 2022.

Alessandro Cortesi OP, is a member of the Italian Roman Province of St Catherine of Siena. Before entering the Dominican Order he studied classical studies at Padua University. Later he studied philosophy and theology at the Angelicum in Rome and completed his doctorate at the Pontifical Institute Augustianum in Rome. He has been a professor at Libera Universita Maria ss Asunta, in Rome, the Angelicum and the Gregorian University where he taught for ten years. After period of administration in the Dominicans he has taught Systematic Theology at the Institute of Religious Sciences (ISSR) Beato Ippolito Galantini in Florecne and since 2009 at the Theological Faculty of Center Italy (FTIC) in Florence. Since 2009 he has been collaborating with Espaces Project of the Dominican Order in Europe and is the director of Espaces Center Giorgio La Pira.

Ulrich Engel OP, a German Dominican friar, is Professor of Philosophical-Theological Boundary Issues at the Philosophisch-Theologische Hochschule Münster, and Director of the Institut M-Dominique Chenu Berlin (Germany).

Gabrielle Kelly OP, is a Dominican Sister. Her early work in education (teacher, principal, SA, Vic) was followed by research and administration in Melbourne and Adelaide Catholic Education Offices. After serving as Provincial Leader of the Adeliade Holy Cross Dominican Sisters (1979–87), she taught English to refugees and tertiary students in SA and overseas, participated in the Justice & Peace and Ecumenical & Interfaith Commissions of the Adelaide Archdiocese Network.

Mark O'Brien OP, an Australian Dominican friar, has been Provincial of his Province and taught Old Tstament in Australia, Pakistan and the UK.

Thomas O'Meara OP, an American Domincian friar undertook doctroral studies in Germany on Paul Tillich, has taught systematic theology at various theological instutions in the USA, Canada and South Africa.

Milton Keynes UK
Ingram Content Group UK Ltd.
UKHW021045120524
442393UK00004B/79

9 781923 006423